boc

A Pair of
Desert-Wellies

SYLVIA SHERRY

A Pair of Desert-Wellies

JONATHAN CAPE
THIRTY BEDFORD SQUARE
LONDON

First published 1985
Copyright © 1985 by Sylvia Sherry
Jonathan Cape Ltd, 30 Bedford Square, London WC1B 3EL

British Library Cataloguing in Publication Data

Sherry, Sylvia
A pair of desert-wellies.
I. Title
823'.914[J]   PZ7

ISBN 0-224-02333-0

Typeset by Columns of Reading
Printed in Great Britain by
R.J. Acford Ltd, Chichester, Sussex

For Ian Carr

CHAPTER

1

"WAVE to him," said Mrs Flanagan. "*Wave* to yer dad!"

"He's not me dad," said Rocky O'Rourke.

"Well – he's yer step-dad – and he's been as good as a real dad to yer, hasn't he? *Wave* to him!"

Rocky pushed his hands into the pockets of his anorak and glared stubbornly out over the grey waters of the river Mersey. Mist was creeping slowly up the river.

"What we're supposed ter wave for, but? *We* can't see him and *he* can't see us."

The oil-tanker moved slowly past them. Mrs Flanagan waved wildly and then sobbed and buried her face in a paper handkerchief.

"Will yer wave like I tell yer, Suzie Flanagan!" she cried to her step-daughter. "It's yer dad goin' off!"

Suzie only gripped the edge of Rocky's anorak.

A thin rain blew into their faces as the tanker slid away towards the mouth of the river.

"Well – he's gone," said Rocky. "Don't know what we had to come down here for."

"Because – because he's gone," sobbed his mother.

"We knew he was goin' last night but," said Rocky, reasonably. "We said terrah to him then. What we doin' here when *he* can't see us and *we* … "

Mrs Flanagan blew her nose hard and got a pound note out of her handbag. "Here, Rocky," she said. "I'm not comin' back home with yer. I can't face it. You and Suzie get the bus back and get some chips and here's the key and mind yer don't put the gas on ter boil a kettle – get yerselves some Cokes."

"Wur *you* goin'?"

"To yer auntie Chrissie's."

"Well, we could come with yer. I've never seen me auntie Chrissie."

"Yes, yer have. Yer've seen her – well yer've seen her twice."

"Flanagan said yer'd look after us when he was away, but yer not – yer goin' off to me auntie Chrissie's. Typical!"

"You mind yer lip and see Suzie doesn't run off. I'll be back tonight." And Mrs Flanagan started away from the Pier Head, her high heels tapping.

"Hi, mam!" Rocky shouted after her. "A pound's no good – there's the bus fare!"

"Oh, all right!" Mrs Flanagan came back. "There's another pound. And I'll want the change."

"Knew he wouldn't last, Flanagan," muttered Rocky. "What's he got ter go away for?"

"Yer know he couldn't get work. He's got ter get some money. Now you get yerselves home, and leave the gas alone!"

8

Rocky and Suzie watched her go away across the car park, and they were alone with the rush-hour traffic swirling round them and the street lamps coming on. Suzie gripped Rocky's anorak tighter.

"S'all right, tatty-'ead," he said, reassuringly. "Yer dad'll be back." He considered things for a moment. "Come on. We'll get the bus home, then we'll get the chips at Chan's, then we'll ... well, come on."

"Two ter Prinney Park," he said to the bus conductor, holding out a pound note.

"You got no change? Don't you know you should have change?"

Rocky looked up into the West Indian face. "You're Beady Martin's uncle," he said.

The conductor frowned. "That's so."

"Well, Beady's a friend of mine. I'm Rocky O'Rourke."

The conductor smiled. "You're Rocky? Well, since it's you, I'll give you change and see you get off at the right stop."

"Thanks very much. And if yer get the bus lost I'll help yer out."

They got off at the end of Princes Boulevard.

"Dark," said Suzie.

"That won't harm yer. Give us yer hand."

They waited on the kerb for a gap in the traffic.

"Should of brought me sleepin' bag," said Rocky. "We'll be here a fortnight." Then he saw the police car and the ambulance parked on the other side of

9

the road, their lights flashing and a crowd of people round. "There's trouble there," he said. "Come on, tatty-'ead!" and he dragged Suzie across.

They wriggled their way through the crowd on the pavement to where a policeman was holding people back and an old, thin woman in a red woolly cap was complaining.

"I live there," she was saying. "In the flats there. And they won't let me in!"

"What's happened, missus?" asked Rocky.

"Somebody's battered old Mr Selby – he lives upstairs to me. Poor soul!"

"Who battered him?"

"Some young thug like yerself!" she retorted.

"Me?" Rocky pushed his hand through his red hair, indignantly. "I'm not ... " But he stopped talking as a stretcher was carried out to the ambulance. The crowd went silent as it passed. The doors of the ambulance were closed and it drove off.

"Poor soul," whispered the old woman. "He'll of been lyin' there in his own blood for hours!"

"Now then," said the policeman. "Nothing else ter see. Let's have the pavement cleared."

"What about me?" The old woman in the red hat pushed forward. "What about me? I live here!"

Rocky pulled Suzie away.

"Dead!" she gasped. "Dead!"

"He wasn't dead."

"Dead!"

Rocky stopped. "Listen, Suzie, I'll tell yer some-thin'. He wasn't dead, see? If he was dead, they would put somethin' over his face. If yer not dead, they don't."

They started off again until Rocky realized Suzie wasn't with him, and looking back he saw her standing with her hands over her face.

"What's up with yer now?"

"Dead!"

"Yer not ... look, Suzie, that's not it. See, yer dead if they cover yer face with a *sheet*. Not with yer *hands*, yer rubbish! Got it? Come on!"

"Not dead, Rocky?"

"I *told* yer!"

Outside number 3 St Catherine's Square, where Rocky lived, Ellen-from-upstairs' baby was propped up in his pram, pink-nosed from the cold and rattling a tin box with some dried peas in it. Rocky gave the pram a friendly shake up and down and the baby, in return, gave him a dribbly grin.

Glad to get in out of the cold, Rocky pulled Suzie into the narrow hall with its ragged linoleum under a dim light bulb and unlocked the door of the first of the two rooms they had. He switched on the light and then the small electric fire. There was a lumpy sofa against one wall and a table in front of it, the bed that Mrs Flanagan and Suzie shared against another wall, two chairs beside the fire and a gas cooker and sink in a dark alcove. It was a cheerless room, but that didn't worry Rocky. He pulled the curtains across the window and fastened them together with the safety-pin.

"I'll geroff for the chips, Suzie," he said. "You stay there. Not be long. All right?"

Suzie only kicked sullenly at a hole in the carpet.

"Yer hear me, Suzie?"

"Me dad's gone," she muttered.

"Well, I *know* he's gone," said Rocky, exasperatedly. "He was all right, was yer dad, but he's gone. Like *my* dad went. But *he* didn't come back." He was just about to explain that *his* dad had died at sea, but he stopped himself. Would only worry her. "But *your* dad'll be back soon, see?" he said, reassuringly.

He watched her anxiously. *His* gang – the Cats – would be waiting for him at Chan's chippy down in Larkspur Lane, but he couldn't leave Suzie in this mood. She was only seven and a queer, silent girl. Ever since she'd come to live with them when his mother married Flanagan, Rocky had been the only one to get on with her, so she was happy with Rocky and would follow him anywhere, racing along with a crumpled bow of ribbon floating from a strand of hair six inches behind her head. But when she got really miserable she would go off and find somewhere to hide – any old corner – an empty house or a hut or the old cemetery beside the Cathedral – and stay there all night. And she looked as if she was in a going-off mood now.

He switched the television on.

"Yer all right, tatty-'ead? Yer'll not run off? Promise."

After a few minutes, Suzie sat down on the floor

in front of the television.

"Right," said Rocky, relieved. "I'll not be long. Yer want mushy peas with yer chips?"

Suzie nodded.

"Yer want Coke?"

She shook her head.

"Well, what *do* yer want?"

"Orange."

"Yer'll not touch the fire?"

She shook her head again.

"I'll have yer hand off if yer do!"

On the doorstep, Rocky paused, scowling across St Catherine's Square, sniffing the atmosphere, sensitive to the mystery and danger of the city at night when anything could happen. The rain had stopped and the last of the sunset glowed over the river Mersey, but it made no impression on the tower of the Anglican Cathedral, which stood out firm and black like a giant head on giant shoulders, peering at him. The Square was dark except for the lights in the old Victorian buildings on three sides and the big block of St Catherine's Buildings on the fourth. Music came from a transistor in one of the houses and from the Buildings came the sound of shouting and some glass being broken. Ellen-from-upstairs' baby had gone to sleep.

Rocky leapt on to the low wall that surrounded the abandoned garden in the middle of the Square, running sure-footed along it towards the street lamp at the corner and the Steps that led down to

Larkspur Lane, where the Cats would be waiting for him outside Chan's chippy.

He was about to jump down the Steps, three at a time, when he stopped. There were two men down there – he could just make them out. One was huddled against the wall and the other one standing over him. Could just be a couple of drunks, but it didn't feel like that.

"No – please – trust me," the man against the wall said, and the other one said, in a quiet, hoarse voice, "Trust *you*, yer dirty grass! Wouldn't trust you with me grandmother, and she's been in her grave twenty years. But *you* can trust *me*!" And he started kicking the man against the wall viciously.

Instinctively, Rocky shouted, "Geroff him!" and the man swung round – and he had a gun in his hand and it was pointed at Rocky. Rocky hesitated only a second, then he put his head down and went like a battering ram at the man, clinging on to his leg and shouting like a maniac, "Drop it! Drop it! Help! He-e-elp!" And the man *did* drop it – he had to while he tried to loosen Rocky from his leg. Then he shoved Rocky hard against the wall, knocking the wind out of him.

When Rocky got to his feet, it was very quiet. He leant against the wall, trying to get his breath back and wondering what he'd run into. Better get back home, he thought. Forget the chips. Then he saw a dark shape lying further down on the Steps. He went towards it cautiously. It was the man who'd

14

been kicked by the gunman.

"Mister. Hi, mister. Yer all right?" His voice sounded very loud in the quiet of the Steps. Heck, he thought, he's had it. But then the man moved. "Yer all right? Was he muggin' yer?"

For answer, the man held out a wavering hand and Rocky grasped it. It was clammy. Holding on to Rocky and the wall, the man slowly stood up.

"I'll get the scuffers," Rocky panted. "Down Larkspur Lane."

"Hold on," said the man, faintly. "Hold on."

Rocky waited anxiously. The mugger could come back. "They owe me, see. The scuffers. I caught this big criminal for them once. He was called Jim Simpson and he was after me brother Joey ... Or I could get Mr Oliver. He's a friend of mine ... "

But the man said, "I'm all right. Not hurt. Not robbed." And he started to climb the Steps. "Must get away ... Help me."

Rocky took his arm and they swayed up the Steps together.

"Get a taxi."

"There's no taxis – 'cept on Prinney Boulevard."

"Help me."

When they got to the lights on Princes Boulevard, Rocky could see the man more clearly. He wasn't very tall and he was fattish and wearing a dufflecoat and his white hair had streaks in it, like nicotine. He was moving his head from side to side, looking for a taxi, and his spectacles flashed each time he moved.

"Yer name?" he gasped. "What's yer name?"

"I'm Rocky. Rocky O'Rourke."

"Saved my life, Rocky."

"Think nothin' of it. I was just on me way ter the chippy, see. Hi, there's a taxi!"

The man waved at the taxi and it stopped. He was getting into it, then he paused. "I owe you a debt," he said, "the biggest any man can owe another." And he put his hand on Rocky's shoulder, and Rocky could feel him trembling.

"I told yer – think nothin' of it. But yer should tell the scuffers. They've got ter earn their livin', see? I could tell them for yer … "

"No. Tell nobody." The man fumbled in his pockets, then handed Rocky a card. "This phone number. Any time – any time you need *anything* – phone this number."

Rocky pushed the card into the pocket of his jeans. "Thanks very much. Yer all right?"

The taxi driver shouted at them, "Are yer gettin' in or are yer finishin' this opera?"

The man ignored him. "I'm trusting you, Rocky. Don't talk about this. And don't give that phone number to *anybody*. Promise me."

"If that's the way yer want it."

"And this … ' He pushed something else into Rocky's hand, got into the taxi and spoke to the driver.

Rocky looked at what he'd been given. It was a twenty pound note! "Hi, mister!" he shouted, galvanized into action and running alongside the taxi as it moved off.

The man pulled down the taxi window. "What is it?"

"S'no good ter me! Never get it changed – can yer not make it ones?"

But the taxi had gone, weaving into the traffic on the Boulevard.

Rocky glared after it in frustration. What a nit! What a nit the man was! Did he not understand? He'd never be able to spend it. Everybody'd think he nicked it! Still, it *was* a twenty. He folded it reverently and put it into his pocket. And I'll get it changed somehow, he thought. And then, thinking of the man with the gun, he pushed his hand through his red hair and shivered. His legs were shaking, his back was sore and he was sweating bullets. He could have been as dead as a kipper by now!

CHAPTER

2

THE Cats gang – except for Little Chan who'd been called in for his supper – was waiting for Rocky outside Chan's chippy. It was a cold October night and Nabber Neville and Beady Martin – one white face, one brown – were huddled against the shop window in the drifting smell of fish and chips. Billy Griffiths, who'd been crippled by polio when he was eight and could only get about easily on his tricycle, sat on it by the kerbstone. They'd been waiting a long time.

"I'm givin' this up," said the Nabber, who was chewing something – the Nabber was always chewing something. "*Wur* is he? He's not comin'. Yer can't trust him!"

Billy wrapped his scarf closer round his neck. His mother would be wondering where he'd got to by this time, but Rocky *had* said he'd meet them there. "Yer can always trust Rocky," he said, quietly. "He's a good skin."

That really started the Nabber off. "Him? A good skin? He's a good skin like you're a good runner!"

Billy didn't reply, but the furrows on his brow deepened. Beady knew he was hurt. "Come off it, man," he said, nudging the Nabber.

But the Nabber was impervious. "It's the truth. Yer remember when he set us up ter break into a empty shop where there was no loot? Brilliant!" He turned to look gloomily in at the two customers in the chippy.

"What d'yer think, Billy?" asked Beady. "I'm goin' ter get battered if I don't get home soon."

But before Billy could reply, Rocky was with them, coming silently out of the shadows in his sandals – his desert-wellies, as he called them – panting hard, his red hair bristling.

"Hi, listen! Youse'll not believe this ... "

"Well yer needn't bother tellin' us. *Wur* yer been?" the Nabber asked, casually. He was feeling very superior in the new camouflage jacket and hat and thick-soled running shoes his father had bought him.

Rocky looked at him, contemptuously. "What's this then? All done up like one of Lewis's dummies!"

Billy limped over to them. "Gettin' late, Rocky."

"Not all that late, wack. Here – look at this ... " As they crowded round him, he pulled the twenty pound note out of his pocket.

"Yer've done some place," said Beady, unbelievingly.

"Let's see it," said the Nabber, putting out his hand to take it.

"Geroff!" Rocky pushed him away. "This doesn't go out of my hands."

"It's not real," said the Nabber.

"Not real? I'll show youse ... "

"Where'd yer get it from, but?" asked Billy.

Rocky paused, looking round at them impressively in the light from the chippy. Then he said, "There was this feller, see. I was comin' down the Steps and he was being mugged and I fought the mugger off and he had a gun and the feller said, 'I owe yer my life' – that's what he said, and 'Get me a taxi', so I got him one and he give me this!"

The Nabber, tall and gawky, leant back against the window of the chippy and pushed his camouflage hat back on his head. "Screwball," he said. "Pull the other one – it's got bells on it."

"I'll pin one on yer, Nabber," Rocky retorted, fiercely. "I'm tellin' youse – there was this man and there was the mugger with the gun and I fought him off and he dropped the gun and he ran off, see?"

The Cats were silent – even the Nabber was silent. It didn't sound real to them, and Rocky *did* imagine things sometimes.

Rocky sensed their disbelief.

"If youse won't believe a twenty pound note, youse won't believe nothin'!" he said, defiantly. "Youse callin' me a liar? Come on. Buy youse all fish an' chips. Youse don't deserve it, but I'll get them. An' yer can eat them at our place. Me mam's out. Buy youse Cokes as well." And he pushed into the chippy and the others followed, doubtful, but fascinated, and determined not to miss this event.

Rocky gave his large order – "Five fish an' chips, four Cokes and a orange."

"You have money for this?" asked Mrs Chan.

Rocky dropped the twenty pound note casually on the counter. "That enough?"

Mrs Chan looked at the note, then at Rocky. There was a streak of dirt down one side of his face and the sleeve of his anorak was torn. She picked up the note and went into the room behind the shop. Little Chan's eldest sister, who was helping in the shop, looked carefully away from them. The Cats were uneasy.

"Wur'd yer really get it, Rocky?" Billy asked anxiously, in a low voice so that Little Chan's sister wouldn't hear.

"I *told* yer! There was this feller ... "

"Yer a nutter if yer think we'll swallow that. This way for the Goon Show!" said the Nabber. "Yer lifted it, didn't yer? Wur d'yer lift it from, but?"

"I'll not tell yer again, Nabber," Rocky began, angrily, but then Mrs Chan came back. "Cannot take it, Rocky," she said.

"It's not pinched!"

"Sorry, Rocky."

"Got to go, Rocky." Billy limped out to his bike.

"See yer, nutter. Come on, Beady."

Rocky's temper flared up. "All right! All right!" he shouted after them. "Yer a rotten lot and youse can keep off me and out of the hideout!" He whirled round to Mrs Chan, glaring at her with tiger-fierce eyes, rubbed a hand through his red hair, pushed the twenty pound note into his pocket and slapped down the pound note his mother had given him.

21

"Two lots of chips, two mushy peas, a Coke an' a orange," he ordered and turned his back on her. "That's what yer get for savin' a man's life," he muttered. "Yer wouldn't believe it!" And he whirled round again and shouted into the room behind the shop, "And if you're in there, Chan, I've had it with you as well!"

Apart from the sizzling of fat in the pans, it was very quiet in the shop when Rocky departed with his chips and his change, and a woman customer who'd taken refuge behind the door when it had all been going on came out cautiously.

"That O'Rourke boy," she said. "He's a real tearaway. He'll go the same way as his brother Joey did and end up in Walton Jail! They're a disgrace ter the neighbourhood, that lot."

Mrs Chan didn't say anything, but swirled some chips round in the pan. And in the room behind the shop, Little Chan, stunned by Rocky's outburst, tried to go on eating his supper.

"Where would Rocky get a twenty pound note from?" asked his father.

Little Chan did not look up from his plate.

"You must not have anything to do with him again. You have better things to do with your time."

Little Chan went on with his supper. He couldn't explain about Rocky to his parents. He would just have to see what happened.

Billy pedalled as fast as he could towards home, relieved when he got to the gateway that led into St

Catherine's Buildings and bumped familiarly over the step at the entrance. He fastened the lock on his tricycle, left it in the hallway and limped slowly upstairs, one hand clutching the banister for support.

"Where've yer been, Billy?" his mother exclaimed when he got in. "Yer dad had to go off to the night shift without seein' yer and yer've had me worried."

"Sorry, mam." Billy sat down to his supper, and after a while his mother said, "Is it that Rocky O'Rourke? He's not got yer into trouble?"

Billy shook his head, but he was worried. He always trusted Rocky – Rocky would never say the things about him that the Nabber said. He was a good skin was Rocky, but Billy couldn't believe in the mugger and the twenty pound note.

Rocky's anger took him straight up the Steps without a thought for the mugger, past Ellen-from-upstairs' baby asleep in its pram and into the living-room of number 3. He slammed the door behind him. Suzie was still mesmerized by the television, squatting on the floor like a little Buddha. She didn't even turn round. What's going on in her head, he wondered.

"All right, tatty-'ead?" he asked.

Suzie nodded.

Rocky disembowelled the steaming parcel of chips and handed Suzie her share and opened her orange. Then he sat on the floor beside her with his chips and Coke. "Yer wouldn't believe it what happened tonight, Suzie," he said, his mouth full of chips.

"That lot – I'm finished with that lot – and there was this man – that's what took me so long, see? I'll tell yer." Then he thought, better not. Might send her off. She wasn't listening anyway. "All right, then, Suzie?" Suzie nodded again.

After all he'd done for them, he thought. Letting them use the hideout, planning break-ins, setting everything up for them, and then they wouldn't believe him about the mugger. If his dad had been alive, if Flanagan had been here, even – *they* would have believed him. *They'd* had experience. And he *had* saved that man's life – that was a fact, and the mugger *could* have shot him. He felt cold just remembering that hoarse, whispering voice.

"Are youse not in bed yet? What d'yer think it is – Christmas?" Mrs Flanagan slammed the door behind her and dropped into her chair. She kicked off her shoes. "Me feet's killin' me. Get yourselves off ter bed and put that telly off. And I'll have me change."

Suzie stood up and stared at her. Rocky picked up the chip papers and empty cans.

"There wasn't no change," he said. "There was the bus fare and the chips and ... "

"Yer haven't gone through two pounds? Wur d'yer think the next two's comin' from with Flanagan away?"

Rocky thought it was best to change the subject. He *had* made a bit out of the two pounds. "Yer see me auntie Chrissie?" he asked.

"Never mind yer auntie Chrissie. She was always a no good."

"What yer mean a no good?"

His mother put on her slippers and sank back in her chair. "Get yerselves off ter bed. And what yer done with yer anorak? It's all muddy and the sleeve's torn. And that's the anorak Flanagan bought yer! Yer want beltin' round the Square for that!"

Rocky took his anorak off and examined it. It *was* muddy and it *was* torn. That was the mugger. No good trying to explain. "It got torn. On some railings. See, I slipped like. It's these desert-wellies. The ridges is all gone. I need a new pair – see ... "
He hopped on one foot after another, lifting his feet up to show the soles of his desert-wellies.

"Yer can give that up!" said Mrs Flanagan. "They're not leakin'. When they're leakin' yer can have a new pair."

"But, mam!"

Mrs Flanagan dropped back in her chair and yawned. "Put the kettle on, Rocky. And you get ter bed, Suzie. I'm wore out."

Rocky hesitated, then he said, "Mam, there was this man on the Steps."

"What yer on about?"

"He was bein' mugged ... "

Mrs Flanagan suddenly sat up, stiff and staring ahead. Rocky and Suzie watched her, apprehensively. They knew what was coming. "I've got the intuitions something awful," she moaned.

Mrs Flanagan's intuitions were well known in the family. They never failed. If she felt something was going to happen – it generally did.

"What yer got the intuitions about?" Rocky asked, anxiously.

His mother stared past him, with a faraway look. "There's trouble comin'."

"She's off again," muttered Rocky, going to fill the kettle and feeling a prickle of fear down his spine. And at that moment there was a knock at the door. The three of them froze. Mrs Flanagan's intuitions didn't usually come right so quickly.

"Who's that? This time of night?" she whispered. "I said it was trouble comin'. It'll be our Joey ... "

"Our Joey? What's *he* got ter do with it? He run off a long time since ... "

"Shurrup!"

They stayed quiet for several minutes, then a voice from outside said, "Police here, Mrs Flanagan. Can I come in?"

Mrs Flanagan shot out of her chair and glared at Rocky. "It's *you* in't it? Not our Joey! What yer been up to?"

Rocky, with the twenty pound note on his mind, backed up against the wall. "Nothin'. I've done nothin'!" he protested.

Suzie disappeared behind the sofa.

Constable McMahon came in. He stood in the doorway and nodded at Rocky. "Glad ter see yer home, lad," he said.

"Home? Where else would he be? Course he's home," said Mrs Flanagan, indignantly. "And what about it? What yer tryin' ter pin on him now? What right yer got comin' into people's homes ... "

"Not come about Rocky, Mrs Flanagan. It's that baby out there in the pram. Bit late for him ter be out. Whose is it?"

Rocky relaxed. "It's Ellen-from-upstairs'. She's not in. There's no light on."

"The poor little thing! He can come in here with us." And Mrs Flanagan went out in her slippers to get him.

"Does she leave him out there late a lot?" asked the constable.

"No. She generally takes him in about five."

"Sure about that?"

"What would I be lying for?"

Mrs Flanagan wheeled the pram in and got the baby out and it started to cry. "There now, luv," she said. "No need to worry, Constable. I'll see to him."

"But where's his mother?"

"She must of been kept back somehow. She'll not be long and he'll be all right with us." Mrs Flanagan sat down, nursing the baby. "Rocky, heat some milk up. He's hungry."

Rocky scowled. "There's no milk. Yer *know* there's no milk. There's only conny."

"Well bring some conny then!" She turned to Constable McMahon. "He'll be all right."

"Leave him with you, Mrs Flanagan." And he went.

Rocky brought the conny, pulled Suzie from behind the sofa and got her into the spare bed in his room. It had been Joey's bed once and his and Joey's room. He'd often stayed awake late at night waiting for Joey to come home so that he could hear all his plans and how he'd done this job and that and how he was in with the big crook, Jim Simpson. But all Joey's talk had been lies, and when he'd run off, Rocky had put a big "For Sale" notice on the wall behind Joey's bed. On the wall behind *his* bed there was a picture of the Liverpool team that he'd cut out of a newspaper and a Star Wars poster.

He switched the light off and got into bed. "All right, Suzie?" he asked. Suzie grunted. But Rocky couldn't sleep. Pictures flashed through his mind – the mugger, the man with white hair, the twenty pound note, Mrs Chan, the Cats. And I'm finished with *that* lot, he muttered to himself. Then he suddenly thought that it couldn't just be a mugger because the white-haired man had said, "Trust me." You wouldn't say that to a mugger. And anyway, a mugger would have a knife – not a gun.

CHAPTER

3

THE first thing that happened next morning was that Rocky couldn't find his jeans. He looked all over for them – in the bed and under the bed and in the cupboard. They'd gone. I've been burgled, he thought. I should of put the money under me pillow. Bet it was the Nabber did it! I'll have him for it!

"Mam!" he shouted. "Wur's me jeans?"

There was no reply, then Suzie wandered in, still half asleep.

"Wur *is* she?"

Suzie shook her head and yawned. Rocky dashed into the living-room. His mother wasn't there. The bed was stripped, there was a pot of cold tea on the table, and no sign of his jeans.

"Wur *is* she?" he asked Suzie again.

"Out."

Rocky was shaken. "Wur's the baby, but?"

"Gone," said Suzie, with some satisfaction.

"Gone where?"

"Gone."

It was unbelievable. The clock on the mantelpiece told him it was only half past eight. His mother never managed to get up before a quarter to nine. "Suzie," he said, urgently, "did *you* take me jeans?"

Suzie looked at him blankly.

The door was pushed open and Mrs Flanagan appeared, preceded by the pram in which, under a large plastic bag full of clothes, was Ellen-from-upstairs' baby.

"Have yer got yer breakfasts?" asked Mrs Flanagan.

"Wur's me jeans, mam?"

"They're in here. I've been ter the launderette. Got everything done. Here," she unearthed Rocky's jeans. "All washed and dried. Get yerself into them and get the breakfasts. Yer'll be late for school."

Rocky grabbed his jeans and went into his bedroom. It was still there in the pocket, the twenty pound note. It was wet and very clean, but still a twenty pound note. Gratefully he smoothed it out. The card with the man's telephone number on it was there as well, though the numbers were a bit blurred. Still, that didn't matter. He got dressed, folded the note and put it into his pocket.

"Are yer not ready yet?" his mother shouted.

Rocky went into the other room. Suzie was at the table eating bread and butter and looking stunned. Ellen-from-upstairs' baby lay on his back on the bed.

Mrs Flanagan picked up the alarm clock and shook it so that it rattled as though all its works were loose – which they were.

"What's the time? We'll have ter get another one of these," she said.

Rocky made himself a jam butty. "What's all this den? What's happenin? Yer've never gone ter the launderette this early before."

"We're goin' ter do things right," said Mrs Flanagan, sitting down in her chair with the bag of washing on the floor beside her. "Just 'cos Flanagan's gone doesn't mean we've got ter let everything go. Now get yerselves off ter school and I'll have a bit of peace. I'm fair laid out."

"I don't believe it," muttered Rocky.

"What d'yer mean yer don't believe it? You mind yer lip – and take Suzie with yer."

"But, mam ... it's me anorak – it's torn."

"Yer anorak?" Gradually Mrs Flanagan's mind focused. "Yer can wear yer old one. I'm not mendin' any anoraks this time in the mornin'."

"But, mam ... "

"I'll not tell yer twice."

Rocky gave up. He put his old anorak on, made another jam butty and said, "Come on, tatty-'ead," and opened the door. Ellen-from-upstairs stood there. "Oh, Rocky," she said. "Wur's the baby? Wur's Trevor?"

"With me mam."

Ellen rushed past Rocky and seized the baby. "Oh, Mrs Flanagan! I've been that worried!"

"He's all right, Ellen. But yer shouldn't of left him. Wur've yer been? The police was here."

"The police!" Ellen sank on to the sofa. "They'll send the social worker! They'll take Trevor off me!"

"They'll do that over my dead body," said Mrs

31

Flanagan. "But wur'd yer get yerself to last night?"

"Was a party," wept Ellen. "Haven't been ter one since I had Trevor. I forgot the time. Couldn't get the bus back and hadn't the money for a taxi."

"Well," said Mrs Flanagan, sympathetically. "Yer only young, after all. But yer should have told me. I would of looked after him. Now I'll make some fresh tea and we'll have a talk." She went to fill the kettle, in charge of the situation. "Are yer not off yet, Rocky?" she shouted.

"Yer mam's real kind," said Ellen, dabbing at her eyes.

"Come on, Suzie," said Rocky.

He turned out of the Square into Princes Boulevard with Suzie trotting beside him, both of them eating jam butties, both of them shivering in the cold wind. Rocky had a quiet, ferocious look. She thinks more of Ellen and Trevor than me and Suzie, he thought.

"Yer know, tatty'-ead," he shouted back at Suzie, "yer'll have ter manage something. Have yer not got a mate at the school would pick yer up and take yer there? I can't keep on doin' this."

After a while, not getting an answer, he looked round. Suzie was standing quite still, several yards behind, and he didn't like the look on her face. He ran back.

"Yer comin', Suzie?"

Suzie shook her head.

"What yer not comin' for?"

"Wrong way."

"It's a *different* way." Rocky scowled. He wasn't going down to Larkspur Lane to meet the Cats as usual. He wasn't having anything to do with *that* lot again! Start up another gang, that's what he'd do. Then he saw that Suzie's eyes were filled with tears.

"What's up with yer? What's der ter cry about?" he asked in desperation, and then pulled the twenty pound note out of his pocket. "Here. See this, Suzie? That's twenty pounds – all in one. Got it? So we're all right, see? An' I'll buy yer somethin' – like a iced lollie – ternight. But yer haven't got ter cry and yer've got to come to school. All right? And yer don't have nothin' ter do with the Cats any more – all right?"

Suzie nodded, seriously.

"And yer don't pick up any half bricks and yer don't run off – all right?"

Suzie shook her head.

"And yer don't hold me hand or I'll batter yer – got it?"

"Stop it! Stop threatening that poor child!" It was the old woman they'd seen the night before – very thin, in old trousers and a raincoat, with straight grey hair and a red woolly cap on top. "You leave that child alone," she said, in a high-pitched voice. "There's too much of that sort of thing."

Rocky was astounded. "What yer on about, missus? She's me sister," he protested.

"More shame on you! I'll have the police here!"

"Look," Rocky protested, "I was only tellin' her … "

At that moment, Suzie, who had been staring at the old woman, came out with a word she shouldn't have. The old woman took a step back.

"Who d'yer think yer talkin' to?" she demanded. "What a thing for a child to say!"

"Belt up, Suzie!" said Rocky. "If yer say that again I *will* batter yer!"

Then the old woman turned on Rocky again. "I know *you*," she said. "You're one of them that did old Mr Selby last night. I know you. You were there."

"I wasn't there! Well, I was, but it was after … "

"I remember seeing you. What did you do with his money?"

"Didn't do nothin' with his money – didn't have his money … "

"I'll report you!"

She must be crazy, Rocky thought. "Yer wrong, missus. Come on, Suzie," he said and started at a trot along the Boulevard with Suzie following, the bow of ribbon in her hair bobbing behind her.

"Witch!" Suzie shouted.

"Der's no witches!"

"Witch!"

At morning break, the Nabber, Beady, Little Chan and Billy got together.

"What's Rocky up to?" asked Beady. "He hasn't said one word to me today."

"He's crazy," said the Nabber. "He's got this twenty pounds and he's gone crazy."

34

"I think he is not our friend any more," said Little Chan, unhappily.

"We don't need him," said the Nabber. "I'm takin' over."

"He said we can't go to the hideout," said Billy.

"Forget that! It's our hideout."

"But Rocky found it."

"Well, it's ours now. He can't stop us using it."

"Hi – he's over there – with Chick and Spadge," said Billy.

The Cats watched unbelievingly as Rocky walked with Chick and Spadge towards Chick's Lot, the gang from Joseph Terrace and the Cats' sworn enemies. Chick and Spadge had been away for some time after they were arrested for doing a flat in St Catherine's Buildings, but there they were back, confident as ever, and Rocky walking between them, smaller than them, but talking a lot. Chick's Lot and Rocky got into a huddle, then Rocky left them and went over alone to the other end of the yard.

"He's gettin' nowhere with them," said the Nabber, triumphantly. "Who needs Rocky O'Rourke?"

But without saying anything, Billy limped over to Rocky.

"Hi, Rocky," he said.

Rocky turned to him. "Hi Billy. All right, wack?"

"Yer not goin' in with Chick's Lot?" Rocky didn't reply. "Rocky, yer can't split the Cats up. Yer can't do it."

"Do what I want. Anyway, youse all left pretty quick last night."

"Was the money – where d'yer *really* get it, Rocky?"

"I told youse, didn't I? It was from the man – he was being mugged – I saved his life – I *told* youse! Only none on youse'll believe it!" Rocky's hair seemed to bristle with anger and he glared across at the Nabber, who was leaning nonchalantly against the wall, grinning.

"Chick's Lot not want yer?" he shouted. "Yer just like your Joey – all hot air!"

Rocky fairly danced with rage. "Put yer eye in a sling if yer don't belt up, Nabber Neville!"

"You and who else's army?" The Nabber stood up straight, glaring back at Rocky, and Chick's Lot grinned and Chick shouted, "Hi! Der's goin' ter be a Cat fight!"

Billy said, anxiously, "*I* believe yer, Rocky."

"Yer've always been a good skin," said Rocky, "and I don't hold nothin' against *you*. But the Nabber's askin' for it – and I wouldn't give much for Chan and Beady neither!"

"I'll talk to them."

Rocky shrugged and turned away. "Please yerself. Doesn't mean nothin' ter me!"

"Hi, Rocky!" Billy shouted after him. "What about tonight – at the hideout? We could have a game of cards – and … "

"Nobody goes into the hideout but me," Rocky retorted, and after a moment's thought he added,

"Anyway – der's no tea and no conny and Suzie's broke one of the mugs."

Rocky stalked away, but Billy, who as manager and secretary of the Cats' football team took notes of everything, got out his biro and notebook and wrote down "Tea conny mug", then he went to consult with the Cats. The Nabber said straight away that he wasn't having anything to do with Billy's plan, but when Beady and Little Chan and Billy got into a huddle about it he changed his mind and took over because, he said, *they* couldn't organize a booze-up in a brewery.

CHAPTER

4

IT was raining again and Rocky went home from school along Princes Boulevard hopping over one puddle after another, because his sandals were leaking. The waterworks should drain this place, he thought. He wouldn't admit it, even to himself, but he was missing the Cats and the talks they always had in Larkspur Lane after school. Only good thing about Prinney Boulevard was the buses that would take you to places – like when his father was at home and they'd go to a match or the Pier Head or the seamen's club together. But his father had died and Flanagan had gone and now the Cats were finished. And Chick's Lot – well, he couldn't go in with them, even if they wanted him. And they didn't. You wouldn't think he'd just saved a man's life and got twenty pounds for it that he couldn't get rid of! Should of been given a medal!

He stood still, brooding over things. His whole life seemed as bleak and battered as the patch of earth in the middle of St Catherine's Square. Then a sudden gust of wind pushed him in the back, rattled an empty can about his feet and sent a damp sheet of newspaper crawling after him like a land crab and he felt better and started to run. He'd get another gang together somehow, and he *did* have the twenty pounds and he would be a famous runner – like Sebastian Coe.

He did a three and a half minute mile – or thought he did – along the boulevard and into St Catherine's Square and only stopped when he found himself in the passage of number 3. He pushed at the living-room door but it was locked. He knocked and shouted to his mother, but there was no reply. Where's she got to now, he wondered, huddling into his anorak to keep warm.

"That you, Rocky?" It was Ellen-from-upstairs leaning over the banister and looking like a mop with her long blonde hair hanging round her face. "Yer mam's out."

"Wur's she gone?"

"Don't know. Could be the 'ousy. Said she wouldn't be long."

"She leave a key?"

"No. She didn't. Yer can come up and wait for her if yer like."

"I'll just hang around."

"She's in a funny mood, isn't she, yer mam?"

Rocky looked up at her. "What yer mean funny?"

"Well, she cleaned all your place and then she cleaned the passage and half-way up the stairs. Then she said she'd had enough and went out."

Rocky looked round. The place *was* clean – very clean. But you could see where his mam had stopped.

"Suzie been back?"

"Haven't seen her, but I wasn't lookin' out for her."

Rocky went out to the front door. Rain fell steadily on the Square, on the trodden patch of grass, the abandoned car and the builder's hut. A lean and hungry-looking black cat was picking its way cautiously over a sodden mess of empty crisp packets, newspapers and take-away trays that had come to rest by the stone parapet round the garden. It stopped to sniff at an empty beer can and then looked up and saw Rocky. They exchanged glances of mutual distrust, then the cat leapt up on to the wall and ran away across the Square.

You would think she would be in when I come home, Rocky grumbled to himself. When Flanagan was here she was always in, but now he's gone she couldn't care less. There's no point in having a clean house if you can't get into it! To console himself he got the twenty pound note out, unfolded it and looked at it. Have to get it changed, he thought. How am I going to get it changed?

From somewhere in the Square he heard a man singing disjointedly, and he made out a lonely figure coming unsteadily towards him. Sometimes it stopped dead, sometimes it twirled round, then it came on again. Rocky knew who it was. His friend, Mr Oliver, the wingy who had once played for Liverpool and then lost an arm in a car accident. He'd been caretaker at St Catherine's Buildings until he was sacked because he was always drunk. But

Rocky had got him another job as caretaker of Mrs Abercrombie's house on the corner that had been made into flats and he'd been doing all right there. Now it looked as if he'd gone on the bottle again. What's up with him, Rocky wondered, and gradually made out the words of the song:

"Every time ... it rains ... it rains
Missiles ... from ... hea-ven
Do-on't you-oo know each cloud's full of
Missiles ... from ... "

Mr Oliver stopped singing to lean for a moment against a lamp-post.

Oh heck, thought Rocky. He *is* drunk. "Hi!" he shouted. "Mr Oliver!"

"Somebody," said Mr Oliver vaguely, "is callin' me ... " and he started off again towards Rocky.

"Yoo'll find di-plaster fallin'
Or'll over the pla-ace –
Ma-ake sure that your humbrella's
Got ar-moured plates ... "

"Mr Oliver," said Rocky.

"The same." Mr Oliver stopped and wavered on one spot. "Hello dur, Rocky. Duck weather, in't it?"

"Thought you was on the wagon."

"Yer right. I was," said Mr Oliver, thoughtfully. "But I fell off. The way things go. You're driving

41

along nice and peaceful and then yer go over a sleeping policeman and the axle breaks."

"What yer on about, Mr Oliver?"

Mr Oliver sat down heavily on the step of number 3 St Catherine's Square and looked gloomily into the distance.

"Yer'll have to give it up, Mr Oliver."

"By what right ... " began Mr Oliver, but Rocky interrupted.

"Youse always tellin' me what I shouldn't do. Now I'm tellin' *you*."

Mr Oliver considered the matter, then he said, "Yer right, Rocky. Yer always is, except when yer not. But yer see, it's the flats. Mrs Abercrombie's flats."

Rocky sat down beside him. "But yer was doin' all right there as caretaker."

"I was, Rocky. I was. Mrs Aber said I was and her nephew – he looks after things – *he* said I was. I got tenants for the first floor – respectable couple, and I got tenants for the ground floor – three nice young fellers, all with jobs, references, rent in advance."

"Never seen them."

"Didn't go out much, except ter their jobs."

"What happened then?"

"Police come yesterday and took the young fellers away – well, two of them. Other one's missin'. Yer can't win, Rocky. The wife's playin' merry hell – she'll have my guts for garters."

"What they done, Mr Oliver?"

"Done? Don't know what they done. Must have done something."

"They must be criminals, Mr Oliver."

"They're criminals all right."

"Well, it's not your fault. You couldn't have known."

"I thank yer, Rocky. Yer a pal. And I'll keep yer advice in mind." He got unsteadily to his feet.

"Mr Oliver ... last night ... "

"What about it?"

Rocky changed his mind. He *had* made a promise. "Nothin'."

It dawned on Mr Oliver that Rocky wasn't happy.

"What's up with yer then?"

"Nothin'."

"I know. Yer dad's gone."

"Not me dad. He's me step-dad."

"Got ter earn his livin'."

"And me mam's out. I'm locked out, see."

"Well, Rocky, I'd ask yer into our place, but yer know what the wife's like. Have to take me shoes off every time I step on the carpet."

"I know, Mr Oliver."

"Well, she'll not be long, your mam."

Rocky shrugged.

"Right," said Mr Oliver, making an effort to be cheerful – and sober, "Cats gang – footy practice – Prinney Park – Saturday mornin' sharp ten."

"Not sure." Rocky couldn't tell him there wasn't a Cats gang any longer.

"Not sure? Yer'd better *get* sure! Get yer team together. I'll be waitin'. Shake on it, Rocky."

They shook hands and Rocky knew what to expect when Mr Oliver shook hands. He felt the coins in his hand – forty pence it would be.

He grinned up at the wingy. "Thanks, Mr Oliver."

"And keep yer chin up."

"What for, Mr Oliver?"

"No idea. See yer, Rocky."

"See yer."

The wingy went off, singing about when it rained. Rocky felt happier. He was a good skin was Mr Oliver, even if he *was* off the wagon and only had one arm. Then he had an idea.

"Hi! Mr Oliver!" he shouted.

"Still here."

"Can yer change a twenty pound note?"

"A what? I didn't give yer a twenty pound note – I give yer forty pence. Didn't I? Must of done. Here – " he dug into his pocket – "see that? Four pounds fifty. That's all there is between me and bankruptcy. Where d'yer get a twenty pounds from?"

"S'not mine," Rocky said quickly. "Flanagan left it with me mam."

"Well, any shop'll change it for her, tell her. She's a lucky woman."

He went away and Rocky sighed with relief. Shouldn't have said anything about the twenty – was a mistake. Mr Oliver had a very suspicious mind.

Rocky considered things. He wasn't sitting there in the rain any longer waiting. He'd go to the hideout. Was *his* place the hideout. And if he found any of the Cats there he'd put them out!

CHAPTER

5

NOBODY – except Rocky, the Cats and Suzie – knew about the hideout. It was the basement of St Catherine's vicarage and Rocky had found it by forcing open the door. Because it was secret, he never went straight into it. He always ran past it, whistling or looking as though he was going to Larkspur Lane for messages, then when he was sure nobody was about, he crept back and shot like a rabbit into its burrow down the steps and into the basement.

The hideout was dark and damp and dirty, but that didn't bother Rocky. It was a second home to him and he always felt safe there. Even in the darkness he could find his way to where the matches were on the old-fashioned range and the candle beside them. When the candle was lit, the hideout looked very comfortable with the old card table, the two kitchen chairs and a stool and the carpet that someone in the Square had decided to throw out. Rocky had seen it beside the dustbins and nipped in and pinched it.

There was paraffin – not a lot, but enough – in the old heater that stood on the range and Rocky lit it, filled the kettle and put it on. The heater gave out no warmth and the kettle would take ages to boil, but the front glowed red and cheerful. Rocky lit another candle.

Was all right, he thought, waiting for the kettle to boil and looking at the postcards the gang had put on the wall – two there from his father when he'd been at sea before he died. Rocky took one of them down and read the message on the back, though he knew it by heart: "Dear Rocky, This is the Southern Cross good ship good voyage Be a good lad Dad." Rocky blinked hard. Things would be different if his dad was still here. He wouldn't have been locked out of the house – and he could have told him straight away about the mugger.

He put the card back on the wall, and then the quietness and emptiness of the hideout began to oppress him. He missed the Cats. But he was finished with them – start a new gang somehow. Could also get some new things for the hideout with that twenty pounds, and some more paraffin.

He turned round quickly. A high-pitched, strange, musical sound had come from the shadows. Rocky froze. Then he shouted, "Whoever's there – come out!" and there was a terrible yelling. For a moment he thought Chick's Lot had taken over the hideout, but it was only the Nabber, Beady, Little Chan and Billy coming out from the corners.

Rocky bristled with anger. "I told you lot!"

"Ah, come on, wack!" said the Nabber.

"I have got this." Little Chan put a packet of Co-op tea on the table.

"Cow-juice," said Beady, putting down a tin of conny.

"This is from me, Rocky," Billy produced a new mug.

"And this," said the Nabber, "is from me." It was a packet of biscuits. "Plenty more where this come from."

"Yer've been lorry-skippin'," Rocky objected. "And yer didn't tell us!"

The Nabber shrugged. "Nothin' like that. There was this box, see, fell off a delivery van outside Pa Richardson's, so I just picked it up, like. Didn't know it was biscuits, but, or I wouldn't have bothered."

They stood around in the candlelight, not looking at Rocky, but waiting. It was an anxious moment. Rocky stood there, frowning hard and thinking. Then he said,

"Right. But it's *my* hideout. I found it."

"That's right, Rocky," said Beady, and smiled.

"And there *was* a mugger."

"We believe yer, Rocky," said Billy and took his spectacles off and polished them.

"And the man *did* give me … "

"A twenty pound note and yer can't get rid of it," said the Nabber. "And are we playin' or are we closin' dis place down?"

"I'm dealin'," said Rocky decisively and sat down at the card table. "Brew up, Beady."

Very much relieved, they got round the table and played cards and ate biscuits and drank tea without speaking. Then Rocky said, "Which of youse was playin' der music?"

"That was me," said Little Chan, with some pride. "It is a Chinese flute. I am a member of the new orchestra at the Chinese centre. It is a very old flute."

"Yer dad not afford yer a new one?" asked the Nabber.

"It *is* a new one. But it is also an old one." Little Chan's brow wrinkled in an effort to explain. "This flute is from ancient China."

"Yer can't have it both ways," said the Nabber. "If it comes from ancient China, it's not new. No way. Dey're coddin' yer!"

"Belt up, Nabber!" ordered Rocky. "And tell yer what, Chan. That flute's goin' ter be our special signal. When we hear it, the Cats get together. Right?"

They all agreed, but Little Chan felt doubtful. His father wouldn't let him take the flute when he went out with the Cats, he was sure. He'd only smuggled it out tonight because it was a special occasion.

After a while Rocky said, "Mr Oliver had the police in. They took two young fellers away from Mrs Aber's flats. Must be criminals."

The Nabber sat back. "Good as havin' muggers," he said.

"I'm tellin' yer, Nabber ... "

"It's true," said Beady. "Was in the *Echo*. They got two, but one got away."

They played in concentrated silence, then Rocky

49

said, "De wingy says footy on Saturday. Can yer get a team together, Billy?"

Billy frowned. "I'll try. There's some tiddlers in Joseph's."

"Tiddlers is no good."

"See what I can do."

"What about yer score of quids?" asked the Nabber. "What'll yer do with them?"

Rocky considered. "Might buy a watch. Yer could get a good one for that. But I think it'll be desert-wellies. Real runnin' shoes with der ridges, you know like. I'm goin' ter be a runner – like Sebastian Coe – "

"Plannin' ter make a quick getaway when they find out where yer got the money from?"

"And that'll fix *you*, Nabber," retorted Rocky, laying down his cards. "My game!" Then he said, thoughtfully, "Know what? Those fellers in Mrs Aber's – they could be the ones did a old man in Prinney Boulevard and took his money. He was took away in an ambulance. Me and Suzie saw it."

The Cats waited.

"Know what? Know what *I* think?"

"Didn't know yer could," said the Nabber, but Rocky ignored him.

"That mugger," he said, "he *could* be the one that got away from the wingy's. Dey was a gang of criminals."

The Cats were hypnotized by Rocky's logic. They had to take him seriously because he'd had experience of criminals. After all, he *had* caught Jim

50

Simpson and *he'd* been a big criminal and had come after Joey.

"Yer'd better look out for the mugger," Rocky went on, impressively. "He's real dangerous. He's got a very thin face and staring eyes – like this!" He opened his eyes wide, sucked in his cheeks and glared round at them. In the candlelight, he looked horrible. The Cats were impressed – even the Nabber was impressed for a few moments, then he flopped back in his chair and pushed his hat back. "What yer charge for hauntin' houses?" he asked.

"Yer can laugh," said Rocky, "but youse've never seen him in action – I have!"

Usually they left the hideout one by one, quietly and cautiously with long intervals in between so that they wouldn't be noticed, but that night, after what had been said about the mugger, it perhaps wasn't strange that Beady and the Nabber managed to leave together, followed by Billy and Little Chan. Rocky was always the last to leave and now he waited in the darkness, thinking about the mugger and the man with white hair. Then he got his courage together, slipped out and closed the door behind him and went soft-footed up the stairs.

There was nobody about in the Square and the light was on in number 3, shining out between the pinned-together curtains. His mother must be home.

He pushed open the door, and then stopped. Everything was clean and tidy! The bed was made and his mother's paper-backed romances in a neat pile at the bottom. The table was cleared and had been wiped down and all it had on it was a vase of paper flowers and a plastic bag of groceries. His mother was sitting by the fire, drinking tea, her hair in curlers.

"What's all this?" asked Rocky. "The Queen comin'?"

"What yer mean comin' home this late?"

"I come home from school and yer wasn't here – the door was locked!"

"Yer should be home earlier."

"How could I be home earlier? They don't let us out till four o'clock!"

"I'm worn out," said his mother. "I've never stopped all day."

"Yer been ter the bingo? Did yer win?"

"Been ter yer auntie Chrissie's."

"What yer want ter see *her* again for?"

"Never you mind."

Mrs Flanagan brooded over her tea cup and Rocky sat down in front of the fire. "I'm frozen. What's there for me tea?"

"Yer'll get it in a minute."

Rocky got up and went to look into the plastic bag. "What yer got?"

"Get yer hands off that. It's not for you. There's a pie heating up."

"I'm sick of pies!"

"Well, yer can like it or lump it. But there's a tin of peas as well," she conceded. Then she sat up.

"Listen, Rocky. I told yer something was goin' to happen. Look at that." She handed him a postcard. It was from Joey. "Back on Friday," it said.

"Which Friday's that?"

"Well – this Friday."

"How d'yer make that out? Could be any Friday. Where's it from?" Rocky examined the card carefully.

"From the Antarctic or somewhere like that – that's where he is. It's a picture of the Antarctic." Which sounded very impressive.

"Well, they must of moved the Antarctic to Blackpool."

"What yer on about?"

"This is the Blackpool illuminations! And it was posted in Birkenhead."

"Here – give us that!" Mrs Flanagan snatched the card and studied it doubtfully. "Well," she concluded, "all it means is he's on his way home. And he'll be here tomorrow."

"Who wants Joey back?"

"What d'yer mean? He's yer brother, remember!"

Rocky did remember. He remembered Joey in his leather jacket with his motor bike and his gang going to do great things – be a big criminal. He'd been Rocky's hero and he'd told Rocky he'd only been sent to jail because he'd been framed by Jim Simpson, a big crook from London. But then he remembered Joey, when he got out of jail, terrified and hiding down in the graveyard by the Cathedral because Jim Simpson was after him and pleading with Rocky to help him to get on a boat that was leaving the Mersey so that he could escape. Was a coward and a liar was Joey, Rocky thought, but he took *me* in. And the mugger was a bigger criminal than Jim Simpson, because Jim Simpson didn't carry a gun.

"That what yer've been cleanin' up and shoppin' for?" he said. " 'Cos Joey's comin'? Don't know why yer bother. We can do without him."

"Yer give that up or I'll batter yer! And wur's Suzie?"

"Was she not with *you*?"

They stared at each other, then Mrs Flanagan cried, "She's gone! She's gone again!"

"Did yer tell her about Joey comin' back?"

"What's that got ter do with it?"

"Yer know she's frightened of him. She was here when Joey belted Flanagan."

"He didn't belt Flanagan!"

"He did – *and* he took yer money. Have ter find Suzie." And Rocky was out again into the dark wet night. Suzie wasn't in the den and she wasn't in the courtyard of St Catherine's Buildings and she wasn't in Larkspur Lane and she wasn't in the builder's hut or the abandoned car.

"She's gone all right," he said to his mother when he got back. "Can't find her. Don't know where she is. Is she with Ellen-from-upstairs?"

But she wasn't.

Mrs Flanagan got up and tied a scarf over her curlers.

"It'll have to be the police," she sobbed.

CHAPTER

6

THE police station in Larkspur Lane was a squat red-brick building with lots of narrow windows. It could have been a run-down Sunday School except for the blue light and "Wanted" notice outside. Time was when Rocky would have run past it shouting objectionable remarks, but that was before he'd caught Jim Simpson for the scuffers. Now he considered he was a part-owner and pushed the door open without hesitation.

Rocky and his mother, in a gust of cold wind, appeared suddenly in the narrow passage and the sergeant looked at them over his desk at the end of the passage in some surprise. "Mrs Flanagan – Rocky – what's to do?"

"It's Suzie!" wailed Mrs Flanagan. "She's gone off again!"

"Yer should keep an eye on that child."

"She's always goin'," wept Mrs Flanagan. "I can't do nothin' with her. There's something wrong with her. With her *head* ... and our Joey's comin' ... "

"Shurrup, mam," hissed Rocky. You should never tell the scuffers nothing – Joey'd been jail-ed once and they could have something on him still. You never knew.

"Well," sobbed Mrs Flanagan. "I'm that worried! Flanagan'll murder me if she's not here when he comes back!"

"Let's have particulars. How long's she been gone?"

Rocky consulted with his mother, and then said, "She come back from school – then she went off."

"That's two hours she's been gone. It's not long. Have yer looked for her?"

"What do *you* think? I've been everywhere," said Rocky.

The sergeant looked down into Rocky's fiercely upturned face. "I'll send a message out to the cars. And if she comes back, you'll let us know."

"The cars?" Rocky was contemptuous. "The cars? What good's the cars? She'll be hidden away somewhere. The cars won't find her. She could be murdered before then."

"Murdered!" Mrs Flanagan shouted. "She's not murdered!"

"Now, Mrs Flanagan ... "

"Oh, come on, mam!" Rocky pushed his hands into the pockets of his anorak, hunched his shoulders and stalked out.

In the Lane he asked, "What did she do, Suzie, when yer told her about our Joey?"

"She started her yellin'."

"Did yer batter her?"

"Give her a slap to stop her. So she run off. Here – where yer goin'?"

"Find her," and Rocky started off along Larkspur Lane.

"Get yerself back quick – our Joey's comin', remember!"

Rocky paused to do a small dance of rage. All she thought about was Joey!

Rocky went all over it again – everywhere he could think of, even down to the Pier Head, though he didn't think Suzie would go that far. But she might. You couldn't tell. The lights over the car park and the bus terminal and the all-night café were blazing away and the café's customers were pressed up against the window watching an old man in an equally old suit and no shirt under it walking backwards and forwards outside and shouting, "Oh, 'ell! Oh 'ell!" at regular intervals. But Suzie wasn't there. She's gone this time, he thought, and started wearily back home. But it was when he was passing the old Rialto cinema at the end of Princes Boulevard that he had an idea. The Rialto was boarded up, but once the Cats had found a broken window at the back and got in – just for the excitement and to have a look round – and Suzie went with them. She could have remembered it.

He went round to the lane at the back – the window was still broken. He hung on to the window-sill shouting, "Suzie!" But there was no reply. Didn't mean she wasn't inside. He ran back home.

Mrs Flanagan was sitting in her chair, looking quite wild.

"Wur've yer been?" she demanded.

"Need a torch," said Rocky and started rummaging among the old clothes, shoes, papers and other rubbish in the bottom of the cupboard. And he found a torch, but it didn't work.

"That's Joey's torch," said his mother. "What yer doin' with it?"

Rocky took no notice. He lit the grill on the cooker and started to take the torch to pieces. He put the batteries under the grill and cleaned the torch. Then he put it all together again, put the batteries back and switched it on. It worked – just.

"What yer doin'?" his mother asked, helplessly, but Rocky was off again, going silently in his desert-wellies to the Rialto.

There was nobody in the lane behind the Rialto. He knocked the broken pieces of glass out of the window with the torch and then listened, holding his breath in apprehension. Still nobody about. He put his hands on the windowsill and heaved himself up. He stepped on to a wash-basin in the ladies' and shone the torch round. Somebody had pulled the other wash-basin away from the wall and smashed it. And at some time, somebody had pulled the door off one of the lavatory cubicles and lit a fire with it on the floor.

He shone the torch round again. There was no sign of Suzie, but there was a pile of stuff on the floor – car radios, cardboard boxes full of tins of salmon, some shirts still in their plastic covers – Marks and Sparks, he thought. All stolen stuff and whoever put it there – this was *their* territory – *their* deri. His skin prickled with the sense of danger and the cold and silence pressed down on him.

Something was written on the wall and he went close, shining the torch up to it. It was scrawled in paint – "Bobby Sissley was here – Bobby Sissley rules – Sissley is the Sissler." Rocky was tense. He'd heard about Bobby Sissley from Chick, and this must be *his* deri. He wanted to get out quick but he had to make sure Suzie wasn't there.

Very cautiously, he pushed open the door that led into the auditorium. The torch didn't make much impression, but it looked as though all the seats had been taken out and there was just a lot of rubbish left – empty cans and crumpled papers.

"Suzie," he said, but his voice came out in a whisper, so he said, as loudly as he could, "Suzie! Yer here, Suzie? It's me – Rocky!"

There was no reply, only a flat echo of his voice – only that vast, empty hall and the small circle of light from his torch – *and* the threat of Bobby Sissley. Rocky was shivering with the cold and the sinister atmosphere of the place. Have to give it up, he thought. Wasn't going to find her this time. She must be somewhere, by herself and terrified, huddled in some dark corner. And anything could happen to her in the streets of that city.

He turned back to the door and then saw something in the dimming light of his torch – a tattered bow of ribbon on the ground. Suzie *must* be there. Then he remembered that when the gang was in the Rialto before, they found a door that led under the stage.

The door, when he found it again, was slightly open. He pushed at it and shone the torch inside. From the darkness there was a scuffling and then Suzie's small face, smudged with dirt, appeared. She looked like a little animal peering out of its lair.

"What yer up to, Suzie?" he asked, angry with relief. "What yer doin' here? What yer want to *do* it for, Suzie? Yer crazy! We've got the scuffers looking for yer – they'll lock yer up! I'm tellin' yer!"

"Rocky," whispered Suzie.

Her voice was tiny as a mouse's squeak.

"What?"

"*He's* comin' back."

"Who?"

"Joey. Don't like him. Don't want to go home."

"Come on – give us yer hand. We're *goin'* home. Forget about Joey. He's not comin' back. And yer'll not come in here again. Promise."

"Promise."

"Dis is somebody else's deri, see. And what d'yer get out of it, Suzie? Runnin' off? I'm warnin' yer – yer'll have ter stop it." But he was sagging with relief that he'd found her.

He was just about to bunk her up through the broken window when he turned round, shining his torch over the wall again. And who was the Sissler when he was out, he thought angrily, spreading himself over the place. There was an aerosol on the

60

floor. Rocky picked it up. He'd leave a message for the Sissler – he'd show him who ruled!

"Can yer write, Suzie?"

Suzie, small and shivering, nodded.

"Can yer get on me shoulders? Want yer to write something – above that writing there, see? Far up as yer can manage. Come on."

He crouched down and Suzie climbed up on to his shoulders. He gripped her ankles and slowly stood up.

"All right, Suzie?"

"Write what, Rocky?" asked Suzie from up above him.

"I'll spell it – big letters, mind. And I'll shine the torch for yer. Write R-O-C-K-Y. Right?"

"Right."

"W-A-S H-E-R-E R-O-C-K-Y R-U-L-E-S. Done it?"

"Done it, Rocky," whispered Suzie. "Go now."

He got her down from his shoulders and shone the torch up to see what she'd written. It wasn't what he'd intended. She'd written, "Rok ws her Rocki rolles."

"All right, Rocky?" Suzie asked anxiously.

"Have to do. Doesn't make much sense, but. Can yer not spell better, tatty-'ead? Still, yer just a tiddler. Come on."

He bunked her up through the window and followed. The lane outside was still empty. He took her hand and began to run.

"She batter me," panted Suzie.

"No, she won't."

"Go away, Rocky. Go away from here."

"Yer daft! Yer have to stay. Flanagan'll be back soon." He paused in the lights at the corner of Joseph Terrace. No sign of Chick's Lot. "Come on," he said, but then Suzie pulled back.

"What yer doin', Suzie? I told yer … " Then he saw what *she* had seen – a gang of tiddlers – they must have been from Joseph's – was dancing round somebody in the light of a street lamp. They weren't making any noise, just dancing round and throwing the occasional milk bottle. And the one they were dancing round wasn't making any noise either. She was just turning round and round with her hands over her head and her shopping bag dangling over her face. It was the old woman in the red hat.

"Bad!" shouted Suzie. She had found a half brick and she threw it. The old woman shouted. The tiddlers stood still, wondering whether they'd found an ally, but suspicious.

Rocky thought fast. "Scuffers!" he shouted, and just as though it had heard him a jam-butty car appeared at the end of the street. The tiddlers disappeared into St Catherine's Buildings and the old woman went on turning round and round, still covering her face.

"Missus!" shouted Rocky. "Hi, missus! Yer all right? Dey've gone."

"Me chicken and chips – I was just gettin' … "

"Well, yer all right … "

She lowered her shopping bag and peered at him. "It's *you*, you little devil! The one that batters his sister!"

"Look – me sister's here … "

"Poor little soul! Poor little soul! *And* yer did Mr Selby. And I've told them. I told the police about yer. Yer won't get away with it!" She went off along the Terrace muttering, "They're all devils – nothin' but devils!"

Rocky was furious. "Next time I'll *help* the tiddlers!" he shouted after her and Suzie went to find her half brick. "Bad," she said.

"Will yer drop that, Suzie? Yer'll have us both in the nick. Come on!"

In the lights of Princes Boulevard, Rocky felt safer and slowed down.

"Not go home, Rocky," panted Suzie.

"Yer *have* ter go home!"

"She batter me."

"She'll not. I'll see ter that. Now … " Suddenly he hesitated. A man passing them had looked hard at him and Rocky thought he knew him – could be the mugger. He looked back. The man had turned and was coming towards them.

Rocky started running, dragging Suzie with him, but she kept on pulling back – "Too fast, Rocky! Too fast!" she shouted. There were some people in the street, but no crowd they could get lost in. And the man was still following.

They got to the phone box about half-way along the Boulevard. Rocky pulled the door open. "Get in, Suzie," he ordered.

"Not get in!"

"Get in – and get down – on the floor."

Suzie got in and sank down under the shelf where there had once been a phone – somebody had removed it a long time ago, but they hadn't removed the light in the ceiling. Rocky reached up with Joey's torch and smashed it. Broken glass sprinkled round them as Rocky crouched down beside Suzie. It was dark in there now – nobody would see them.

"Game," Suzie murmured, happily. "Game – hide – game – hide-game. Not go back."

Suddenly the phone box seemed darker. Rocky twisted round. A man stood outside, two hands pressed against the glass, a narrow, fierce face with eyes in dark sockets, watching them. They were trapped.

It was then that Suzie saw the man and started screaming.

When the jam-butty car stopped by the kerb, the mugger had gone. A policeman pulled open the door of the phone box and Suzie stopped screaming.

"What's up, then?" asked the policeman.

Rocky took a deep breath. "Nothin'," he said.

"You'd better both come out."

"I'm Rocky O'Rourke," said Rocky, quickly. "I was just phoning the station at Larkspur Lane. You'll be lookin' for my step-sister – she got lost. This is her. Suzie Flanagan. I've found her. You can call the search off."

"Where did you find her?"

"Upper Parly Street. She'd got lost," Rocky lied.

"She all right?"

"Oh, Suzie's all right. Just got lost like."

"I'll take you both home."

Rocky hesitated. He would have felt safer in the police car, but he knew he'd never get Suzie into it.

"Der's no need. We know the way. And it's not far – St Catherine's Square. If you could tell the sergeant at Larkspur Lane she's all right, see?"

"Go on then. We'll follow you – see you get home. You're a clever lad," he added, "phoning from a box with no phone in it."

"Trust a scuffer!" Rocky muttered as he grabbed Suzie's hand.

Mrs Flanagan saw them coming. She was out on the pavement looking anxiously round the Square. "Yer've got her! Wur was she? I'll take the hide off her!"

Suzie got behind Rocky.

"Yer'll not touch her. She's frightened."

"Where's she been? She needs a lesson."

"If yer don't promise yer won't batter her we'll both run off."

Mrs Flanagan gave in. "Get yerselves inside. I'll go and tell the police she's back."

"I've told them."

Ellen-from-upstairs came along, all smiles. "Hello, Mrs Flanagan," she said, lifting Trevor out of his pram. "Yer all right? Will yer wheel the pram in, Jack?" she said to the young fellow with her.

Mrs Flanagan gave them a hard stare as they went

upstairs. "She's late back again! She'll come to no good that one," she muttered and went into their living-room. She looked at herself in the mirror over the mantelpiece and then sank into her chair. "I can't go on with this," she said. "That child's got me wore out with her carry on. I've give her a good home and she's not mine, after all. Something'll have to be done. She'll have to be got into a home till Flanagan comes back."

Rocky took no notice of his mother's grumbles. He was tired and hungry. "What's there to eat?"

Mrs Flanagan sighed. "There's that pie – and then get yerselves ter bed."

"I'm not havin' that pie." Rocky began to investigate the contents of the plastic bag that was still on the table.

"You leave that alone! That's for Joey."

"He's not come back den, our Joey?"

"Not yet. But he'll be here. I don't know. I do me best. I've washed and I've cleaned and I've shopped and then Joey doesn't come and *she* has to worry the life out of me and the police … "

Suzie backed up against the door, but Rocky skilfully and silently extracted two packets of crisps from the plastic bag, nodded to Suzie and went out to his bedroom. He got Suzie into bed and gave her a packet of crisps, got himself into bed – carefully putting the twenty pound note and the man's card under his pillow – and opened *his* packet of crisps. For a while there was nothing but the sound of crunching.

Then, "She not batter me," said Suzie, happily.

"No – but don't do it again."

"*He* not come."

"He'll not be coming. All hot air is our Joey."

"You buy me doll."

"Tatty-'ead, if yer don't go to sleep, *I'll* batter yer!"

Suzie dropped her empty crisp packet on the floor, wriggled under the blanket and fell asleep.

Rocky lay awake a long time, wondering what to do. It *had* been the mugger that had come after them. Rocky couldn't be wrong about those eyes and that face. But what was he coming after them for? Couldn't be for the twenty pound note – he couldn't know about that. He couldn't be just a mugger. It had to be something else. Something worse. He turned over restlessly. No good telling his mother about it – she wouldn't believe him. And Mr Oliver – well, how could he explain things to Mr Oliver?

"Bad! Bad!" Suzie shouted, suddenly, in her sleep.

"Shurrup, Suzie!" he whispered, urgently, and Suzie muttered, turned over and was quiet.

CHAPTER

7

IT was hardly light when Rocky woke up and Suzie was still fast asleep. He got dressed quietly and put the twenty pound note and the man's card into his pocket. *And* the forty pence he'd got from the wingy. Then he went cautiously into the next room. His mother lay in a shadowy huddle on the bed, but a beam of light from the street lamp outside slanted through the pinned-together curtains on to the bag of groceries still on the table. The plastic bag rustled as he felt inside and got out a packet of biscuits, and the wrapping on the biscuits made an even louder noise as he extracted half a dozen. But his mother didn't stir. He went out of the house munching them.

A cold wind was blowing round the Square and the sky was lightening into a pale grey. And there was nobody about yet. Rocky pushed his hands into the pockets of his anorak and leapt on to the wall round the garden and ran along it towards the Steps. He paused for a moment at the top to make sure the mugger wasn't there, then he ran down to Larkspur Lane. Two men walked along quickly on their way to work and a car was being revved up somewhere.

The tower of the Anglican Cathedral was black against a luminous sky. Pa Richardson wasn't open yet and Chan's chippy wouldn't open till eleven o'clock. The snack bar sometimes didn't open at all. And the small, mysterious shop with its dirty window decorated with dead flies and full of sun-faded blankets and children's clothes was still a blank except for the pale oblong of the notice that was always stuck in the window and which Rocky knew had written on it, "Goods laid aside". Apart from the street lamps and the police station, the only other light came from the newsagent's shop – and that was hesitant.

Rocky got into the phone box and dialled the man's number and heard the phone ringing. Then a voice said, "Hello?" and Rocky put in a ten-pence piece.

"It's me – Rocky – Rocky O'Rourke ... Is that ... "

"Yes, Rocky."

Rocky relaxed. He recognized the voice. "Hi, mister – it's the mugger – he's back."

"Go on."

"Last night – Prinney Boulevard – he come after me ... "

"Sure it was him?"

"Certain. And he was comin' after me – but what would he be comin' after *me* for?"

There was a pause and Rocky asked anxiously, "Yer still there, mister? 'Cos this is costing me ten pence and ... "

"Listen, Rocky." The man's voice was quiet and

69

steady. "You're sure it was him?"

"Certain, but ... "

"He's only coming after you to get me ... "

"But mister ... "

"If he comes again, get out of his way and phone me straight away."

"S'all right talkin' but he could cut me throat, couldn't he? And then I couldn't phone yer. And I want out of this and there's this twenty pounds – I can't change it and ... " But the line had gone dead.

Big deal, Rocky thought. All he's done is drop me in it! It's not a mugger. Can't be. *Must* be something worse. There were one or two more people in the Lane hurrying to work and none of them looked like the mugger, but Rocky felt vulnerable. He'd have to watch it – keep with the Cats as much as possible and not be on his own. Then suddenly he whirled round and did a Kung Fu kick. Then he lashed out with a karate chop. Then he grabbed some fresh air from behind his shoulder and threw it on the ground in front of him. Then he started running and came up sharp in the newsagent's.

The woman behind the counter, who'd seen this pantomime, asked coldly, "You got a holler head?"

Rocky, not sure where he was because he'd just been fighting off an imaginary attack by the mugger, glared at her. She was weird – arms like bird's legs sticking out of a sleeveless blouse and a red gash of a mouth with a cigarette in it. Must be new here, he thought. Seen better faces on clocks.

And he turned to the stand where the comics were and pretended to be looking for one. His mind was still on the mugger, but it was safe in the shop and he got engrossed in a story in the *Eagle* because it was about a victim in a similar situation to his, only *he* was having trouble with an Alien, not a mugger. Rocky had just got to the point where the Alien was sucking out the entire contents of the victim's brain when the woman snapped, "Yer buyin' that? Because this isn't the Picton Library!"

"Not worth buyin'," Rocky retorted and turned his back on her. He wanted to know what happened to the victim, but he'd only got thirty pence left and the *Eagle* cost twenty. It would leave him nearly bankrupt. Swiftly, he slipped the *Eagle* inside a copy of the *Dandy* – which was only ten pence – and waved it at the woman.

"I'll take this one, but," he said, and dropped ten pence on the counter and got out fast. That would show her who'd got a holler head!

The Cats were looking in at the tins of baked beans and tomato soup and packets of biscuits in Pa Richardson's window and Pa Richardson was looking out at *them* suspiciously.

"Hi!" Rocky ran across to them, pushing the comics down the front of his anorak.

"Return of Superman," said the Nabber, sarcastically.

"Put a trap on yer moey, Nabber Neville!" retorted Rocky. Then he saw there was something different about Pa Richardson's – it was the iron grid over the window. "What's he got that there for?"

"Thinks he'll be done – by you – or Chick's Lot – and he's right there."

Rocky hunched his shoulders and started along the Lane with the Cats following. They were a bit anxious, because Rocky said nothing. Even the Nabber was a bit anxious.

"All right, Rocky?" asked Billy, cycling alongside.

"All right, skin." But Rocky said no more for a while, his mind being on a lot of things. Then, "Hi," he said at last, "there's this story in the *Eagle* about a Alien that sucked out the entire contents of his victim's brain. It's smashin'!"

"Sucked out his brain? Ugh!" And the Nabber gave a good imitation of somebody being sick all over the pavement.

"Not his *brain*, the *contents* of his brain. That's his thoughts and all that. And a Alien wouldn't bother with yours – yer've nothin' in it! And listen." He stopped suddenly. "Chick and Spadge won't do Pa Richardson. They're straight now. They told me."

"Coddin' yer," said the Nabber.

"It's the truth. They don't want ter be taken in again, see? Next time they'll get longer, see? They say it's not worth it. But they told me – somebody else's taken over Joseph's. And *he'll* do Pa Richardson's."

"Who's he then?" asked Beady.

"He's called the Sissler," said Rocky grimly.

"The Sissler?" The Nabber stood still. "The Sissler? First it's the mugger, then it's a twenty

72

pound note, then it's a Alien, then it's the Sissler! It'll be E.T. next! Yer must of lost yer marbles."

"Yer know nothin', Nabber Neville," and Rocky walked on with the air of someone who had state secrets on his mind. "Last night, see, our Suzie run off an' I found her in the Rialto and in the ladies' – where there's the window broke – it was somebody's deri and there was written up all over the walls about Sissley being the Sissler. And rulin' and all that. And lots of loot lying round. All kinds of gear. Tellin' yer." The Cats watched him warily until he stopped at the school gates.

"And somethin' else happened. Was the mugger. Followed me and Suzie on Prinney Boulevard."

The Cats expressed no disbelief – they didn't dare to after Rocky's reaction in the chippy about the twenty pound note. They just stood around, thinking maybe he *had* lost his marbles. Then the Nabber said, sympathetically, "If it gets too bad, yer know like, they can always take yer into the loony-bin and give yer electric shocks."

"I'll jump on yer head yet, Nabber!" Rocky shouted.

"Come on den – try it!"

"It is five minutes past nine," said Little Chan, quietly, and went through the school gates.

"Have to go, Rocky." Billy cycled after him.

Rocky made his mind up. If the Sissler could get his own deri and all that loot, *he* could get a twenty pound note changed, *and* he could do the Sissler's deri, *and* he could ... "I'm saggin', Beady," he said,

73

ignoring the Nabber. "Yer comin' downtown?"

Beady shrugged. "There's no percentage in it. Me mam'll just batter me. Come on, wacks."

Rocky glared at him. "Right lot of ... "

"What yer got lined up?" asked the Nabber, interested.

"Get some desert-wellies."

"I'll sag with yer."

Rocky didn't say so, but he was pleased to have the Nabber's company. "That lot's got no guts," he said, implying that the Nabber had.

"Don't need them, but," said the Nabber. "They haven't got a mugger and a Alien and the Sissler." He obviously meant this as a compliment and Rocky accepted it as such.

"My dad", the Nabber went on, "knows a feller works in one of the shops downtown. If yer give him three pounds he'll let yer have a pair of shoes – any kind. See, he takes the three pounds, but he doesn't put it through the till."

"He'll take the twenty pound note?"

"Not think twice about it."

"Yer sure about this feller?"

"Course I'm sure. My dad *knows* him."

"Yer dad had shoes off him?"

"Course he has!"

The Nabber stopped and turned round. Suzie was just two yards behind them. "*She's* not comin' with us!"

"Go to school, Suzie!" Rocky commanded, but Suzie didn't move.

"She can come," said Rocky. "She'll be no trouble."

"We can't go downtown with *her!*"

"She'll be all right. Won't yer, Suzie?"

"Yer mean yer can't get rid of her!"

Suzie stared at the Nabber. "Don't like *him*," she said.

"Forget it, Suzie. Come on."

"First time," grumbled the Nabber, "I've sagged school and gone downtown with a tiddler!"

As they got off the bus, Rocky said – because he *had* to tell somebody, "Hi, that man with the white hair, yer know like – phoned him this morning."

The Nabber stopped chewing for a moment to ask, "What'd he say? Hello?"

"He *said* the mugger was comin' after *me* ter get ter *him*."

The Nabber said nothing.

"Yer don't believe me!" said Rocky fiercely.

"I do believe yer!" protested the Nabber. "Yer couldn't have invented it – that would take brains and the Alien got yours, didn't he?"

Before Nabber knew what was happening, Rocky had dropped behind him, pushed him in the back with his right hand and put his left foot round Nabber's left foot and pulled.

"What yer want ter do that for?" asked the Nabber, sorrowfully, sitting on the pavement among the feet of the passers-by.

"I didn't do nothin' – was the Alien," said Rocky, innocently. "Did yer not see him?"

CHAPTER

8

"Which is it? The shop with this feller?" Rocky stopped, looking down the line of shoe shops.

The Nabber shrugged. "Not sure. We'll just try some, like. I'll know him when I see him."

"Yer mean yer don't know. Typical! I'll just buy some!"

"Yer've changed the twenty?"

Rocky didn't intend going into that.

"Come on," said the Nabber, "where'd yer really get the twenty from?"

"I *told* yer! There was this feller ... "

"Yer saved his life. All right. Yer thought up a good one there."

"I'm not tellin' yer again, Nabber!"

They looked into several shops, but Nabber was never certain which was the one with the man who'd sell you a pair for three pounds. At last, Rocky stopped at a shop with a lot of desert-wellies on a rack outside. He tried some on. "This is all right," he said at last. "This is the right size."

"How much?"

"Thirteen pounds! It's a rip-off!"

"Yer've got the money, but."

Rocky hesitated, but he knew the reaction he'd get to that twenty pound note. "I'm not payin' thirteen pounds", he declared. "Look, these ones is all right feet. We could find some left feet outside another shop and then I've got a pair free. Doesn't matter, yer know like, if they're different colours." The Nabber thought it was a good idea and he would have a pair as well. But they couldn't find any left feet – all the shops had right feet on display.

"It's a conspiracy," said Rocky at last. "They saw us coming."

"I'm goin' off it," said the Nabber. "Are yer buyin' or are we goin' down here till we fall into the Mersey?"

Rocky made his mind up. "Come on. I'm givin' it up. Buy yer a cup of tea in Lewis's. And we'll be foreigners – all the way up Bold Street. Suzie ... "

Suzie had her pockets stuffed with odd shoes. Hastily Rocky pulled them out and dumped them. "Will yer give it up, Suzie. I'll batter yer! She's a proper liability."

"Why don't yer lose her in the Tunnel?"

"Yer couldn't lose Suzie in the Tunnel. She'd just walk through to Birkenhead and get a lift back. She's not daft!"

"Yer could of fooled me!"

They started back, jabbering to each other in what sounded like a foreign language. Rocky sounded a bit Chinese and the Nabber sounded a bit Spanish and they pushed through the crowds, gesticulating, stopping in front of some buildings and looking up at the roofs and had people staring at them. They got to Lewis's and collapsed in the doorway, laughing.

"Hi! They thought we was foreigners!"

"Come on – buy yer a cuppa." They went into the cafeteria. Rocky had enough money for a cup of tea each.

"What about *her*?" asked the Nabber.

Solemnly, Suzie got herself a plastic cup of orange juice and went like a duck below the counter and past the check-out point.

"She's a born criminal," said the Nabber.

"She's not bad at it," Rocky conceded.

They sat drinking tea and talking foreign and watching Suzie pour vinegar into the pepper pot until a waitress came up.

"Finished?" She started to clear the table. "What's wrong with youse?" she asked. "Who d'yer think yer coddin'? And why yer not at school?"

"We're too old," said Rocky. "We're too old," he went on in a quavering voice. "Help me up, Nabber ... " And they left the cafeteria, leaning on each other, shaking and speaking in weak voices with Suzie trailing behind.

They gave that up when the Nabber decided he would help himself to a couple of badges from one counter and Rocky got some batteries for Joey's torch from another. They'd just got together again and were going out of the shop when a manager appeared.

"Come on, you two. Out," he said.

"We're goin' out. What's up wid yer? We've done

78

nothin'," Rocky protested, immediately.

"Out."

"We was just havin' a cup of tea."

"What's that in your pocket?" And the manager extracted two batteries from the pocket of Rocky's anorak. "These paid for?"

"No," said Rocky, innocently. "They fell off the counter, see? I was takin' them back."

"If it wasn't too much bother, I'd have the police in. Now you two are barred from this shop!"

"That's what happens when yer honest," objected Rocky, and they left the shop in a dignified way and then collapsed laughing.

"Hi – I needed those batteries but," said Rocky. "Get them again. Come on!" He grabbed Suzie and they crossed the road and ran up Hardman Street.

They got on to a bus, heaving Suzie up after them, and made for the upstairs.

"Now, Rocky, where you goin'? I have to have some money from you," the driver said.

Rocky turned back. "It's Beady's uncle," he explained to the Nabber. "We just want a lift, yer know like," he said, cheekily.

"I don't give lifts."

"But Beady – he would want yer to ... "

"This bus will not start until I have your fares."

Rocky shrugged. Worth a try, he thought. "Got some money, Nabber?" Between them they found enough for the fare and clattered noisily upstairs and subsided. After a while Rocky said, "That deri – the Rialto."

"What about it?"

"It's the Sissler's – no question. And all that stolen stuff – must be worth a lot." They contemplated this, then Rocky went on, "How's he get rid of the gear, the Sissler?"

"That's easy," said the Nabber. "There's lots of people'll take it – there's a woman in St Catherine's Buildings – she'll buy anythin' off yer."

"Like the man in the shoe shop that'll sell yer … " Rocky began scornfully.

"*He* must of moved on. They do, yer see. They move on. Anyway, *she's* still there."

"Believe it when I see her." Rocky contemplated the world outside the bus window for a while, then he said, "Funny in't it?"

"What is?"

"Nobody's never seen the Sissler – except Chick and Spadge."

"Nobody's never seen the mugger – except you!"

"What yer gettin' at?"

"Nothin'," said the Nabber, quickly. "Nothin'!" Then he added, "D'yer think the mugger's a relative of the Alien?"

They had a minor, unserious punch-up after that and then stampeded down the stairs and got off. As the doors of the bus closed, Rocky realized Suzie wasn't with them and hammered on the bus door. Beady's uncle opened it. "Forgotten something, Rocky?"

"Me sister!" He ran upstairs and found Suzie sitting there, oblivious. "Come on, tatty-'ead! Yer going home, not ter Runcorn!"

They crossed Princes Boulevard.

"Terrah then, wack," said the Nabber. "Thanks for the tea."

"Thanks for gettin' me the desert-wellies," replied Rocky, sarcastically.

"Think nothin' of it. Do it for any skin. See yer!"

"Hi, Nabber!" Rocky shouted after him. "Keep it in mind – the Rialto!"

The Nabber waved in agreement.

Outside Mrs Abercrombie's, half a dozen people were being shouted at by the wingy. "Will youse clear off! There's nothin' more ter see. The show's over!"

"What's goin' on, Mr Oliver?" asked Rocky.

"Been like this all day. They think this place is Madame Tussaud's and they've got me down for Jack the Ripper!"

"Is it them young fellers yer took in?"

"The ones I took in? Yer mean the ones that took *me* in! The police come back and had the floorboards up – *and* they'd just been put in new. They found some guns – and some dynamite. Had a dog with them sniffing it out. S'been merry hell all morning!"

Rocky was impressed. "Yer could of been blown up!" he said, with some relish.

"Yer don't need ter tell me. How was I to know what they was up to? How was I ter *know*?"

"Yer couldn't, Mr Oliver. It's not your fault."

"Thanks, Rocky. Yer a pal. I mean, yer know

like, they was that quiet – no parties nor nothin'. Only one that ever came ter see them was an uncle of one of them – white-haired feller, very soft-spoken. How could I know they was turning the place into a bomb factory? I can't get over it, Rocky. But I'm in the clear. The police clarified me. McMahon put in a word and the Abercrombies is keepin' me on. Wife's had hysterics all day, but apart from that", he finished gloomily, "everything in the garden's lovely."

"Mr Oliver," said Rocky, suddenly anxious, "what was he like? The one that got away?"

"Him? He was weird – thin fellow with a funny voice. Didn't say much, but he could give me the creeps just lookin' at me. Always thought he could of scared corpses stiff in a cemetery. Reminded me of a centre-forward we had on the team – always scored when he got the ball. Wasn't all that good – just terrified the opposition by lookin' at them."

Mr Oliver leant his one arm on the gate reflectively and started recalling other footballers he'd known, but Rocky didn't hear him. He was back on the Steps with the white-haired man and the mugger. He could hear their voices – "Trust me!" – "Trust *you*, yer dirty grass." There was no question they were the terrorists from Mrs Aber's and *he'd* saved the white-haired man's life, so the man with the hoarse voice would come back for him. He was the pig in the middle – he knew it.

Mr Oliver's voice came to him – "Yer gone stone-deaf?"

"What's that, Mr Oliver?"

"What you and Suzie doin' out of school this time of day?"

"Half-holiday," Rocky said, not thinking, because his mind was on the terrorists.

"Half-holiday? What for? Here, wake up, Rocky!"

Rocky thought quickly. "Somebody's birthday. Suzie's."

Mr Oliver looked surprised, but Suzie caught on quick and nodded and smiled. "They give the school a half-holiday … "

"No, Mr Oliver. Only me mam asked if we could have it."

"Havin' a party?"

"Just a tea – and some cakes."

"Well, then," said Mr Oliver, "happy birthday, Suzie! And shake." Hesitantly, Suzie held out her hand to Mr Oliver and felt some coins in it. She looked up at the wingy with a dazed smile, then pulled a doll out of her anorak. "Barbie!" she said.

Rocky stared at it. She must have nicked it from Lewis's, but he hadn't seen her doing it.

"That a present, Suzie?" asked Mr Oliver. "Yer a lucky girl, aren't yer?"

Suzie shook her head. "Take," she said, holding up the doll. Suzie was always honest.

"*I* don't want it. It's yours."

"Take," repeated Suzie, getting into the swing of things.

The wingy looked sharp. "What's she mean, Rocky?"

"Just bein' friendly," said Rocky, quickly, but Suzie shouted "Take!" and waved the doll about.

"What she talkin' about? What yer been up to?" Mr Oliver sounded suspicious. "I hope yer've not been … "

"Not been up ter nothin'. Have ter be goin'. Come on, Suzie," and he started to drag her away, but she kept on waving the doll and shouting, "Take!"

Mr Oliver came a few steps after them. "Rocky, I want a word … "

But Rocky didn't stop. Mr Oliver had a very suspicious mind and Suzie wasn't helping. Shouldn't have let her lift the doll, he thought. Should have watched her. It was all right him and the Nabber nicking things, just for the excitement – made yer sweat. But Suzie didn't understand it. And what would happen to her if the scuffers found out? That made him sweat.

"Listen, Suzie," he said sternly, "yer haven't got ter take things, see? If yer do, they'll put yer in a home."

That seemed to cheer Suzie up. "Home," she said, "Warm, cakes, toys … Put you in home as well. Warm, cakes, toys … " It was becoming a chant and he said quickly, "Yer wrong, Suzie! S'not like that! Der'll be no cakes and no toys. An' it'll be *cold*!" He nearly added that Joey would be there – just to really frighten her, but then he thought better of it. And anyway, Suzie was frightened enough. "Not go to home! Go away!" she sobbed.

Then he was worried that she might go off again.

"Listen, Suzie, yer'll not go ter the home this time, see? But yer keep that doll hidden. Stuff it down yer anorak. And yer don't do it again, got it?"

Suzie sniffed and wiped her nose with the back of her hand.

"Come on, then." He started for home, but Suzie held back.

"Cakes," she said.

"Der's *no* cakes!" he said, exasperatedly.

"Birthday!" Suzie sobbed.

Rocky was desperate. Once Suzie got her mind on something ... Then he had a thought. "What'd he give yer, Suzie? The wingy?"

She held out her hand. "Fifty pence! He's never give me more than forty. Still, it's supposed ter be yer birthday. Secret birthday, Suzie. Just us two knows about it. Come on."

They burst into Pa Richardson's and Pa Richardson took one look at them and said, "If yer don't mind – sniff – Mrs Anderson, I'll just see to these two first – sniff – yer never know what they're up to. Now then. And will yer – sniff – tell yer sister to get her hand out of them sweets?"

Rocky ignored this – he had the money, after all. "What yer want, Suzie?"

Suzie didn't have to think about it. "Ten frogs an' toads and a watch."

Cautiously, Pa Richardson counted out five yellow frogs and five black toads into a bag and added one watch.

"That it?"

"And two of them cakes."

"What yer payin' with?"

"Money," said Rocky, slapping down the fifty pence, "unless yer takin' bottle tops!"

They drank tea and ate cakes in the hideout and watched the legs of passers-by through the window. Suzie played with the doll, admired her watch and at intervals put a yellow frog into her mouth, followed by a black toad. When she'd finished them, she started on the watch.

The candle seemed to get brighter as the hideout grew shadowy around them and Rocky, thinking about the terrorist who would be coming after him, thought they'd better get home before it got really dark.

"Come on, tatty-'ead. Yer've had yer party," he said.

As they got into the Square, Suzie suddenly gripped his hand tighter. "Man!" she whispered, and a man *was* walking across the Square – a thin man, walking quietly. Suzie was nobody's fool, Rocky knew. The man reminded her of the terrorist outside the phone box. They stood still and waited. The man went past, not seeing them, and Rocky dragged Suzie across to number 3.

CHAPTER

9

"GET into it! Follow it through! Come on – yer've got the wind with yer!" yelled the wingy and in Princes Park, under a steel-grey sky, Suzie, nearly blue with cold, jumped up and down shouting enthusiastically but incoherently as Little Chan passed the ball to Rocky who sent it out to Nabber who kicked it several yards to the left of the goal-post (which was Billy's jacket) and Beady fell full out on the grass in an unnecessary attempt to defend the goal.

The wingy blew his whistle. The Cats team, which was the Cats gang with several others recruited from the Square and the Buildings, stopped playing.

"Right. All of youse. Over here."

They walked reluctantly towards Mr Oliver in their red shirts. Red was the Cats' colour and was displayed in all shades from red to orange. Rocky, in a near purple shirt that clashed horribly with his red hair, spent a bit of time dribbling the ball round and kicking it up and down several times off his foot, just to show he could do it.

"*When* yer ready," said Mr Oliver, and Rocky

picked up the ball and joined them. Suzie pushed her way to the front so that she could look up into Mr Oliver's face and listen intently to what he was saying, but without understanding a word.

"I've seen nothin' like it. Not in a lifetime. Where's yer eyes? Where's yer feet? Where's yer *brains*?"

"It's Nabber's fault," said Rocky. "Chan and me got the ball to him, but he messed it up."

"Was in the wrong place – nothin' yer could do with it," retorted the Nabber.

"Go on! Yer a toffee-foot!"

"I'll toffee-foot yer!"

"They haven't all played together as a team before, Mr Oliver," said Billy, apologetically. "They just need some practice."

"They need some competition. Now, Billy, have yer got a match lined up? What about Chick's Lot?"

"They always beat us, but," said Beady. "They're bigger and they bring in the Crown Street gang and they play dirty."

"Not while I'm ref," said the wingy. "Billy, you're manager. Can you arrange a match – next Saturday. That'll give us a practice tomorrow."

"Do me best." Billy made a note of it.

"Yer not worried about goin' into Joseph's to get it set up?"

"Been all right up ter now."

"And what about you?" The wingy turned on Rocky. "What yer doin' as captain?"

88

Rocky scowled. "Can't do much with this lot."

"It's a bad workman that blames his tools."

That went home to Rocky. His father had always said that.

"Got a lot on me mind just now," he muttered, which was true.

"Such as what?"

Rocky looked away. Mr Oliver was a bit of a mind-reader.

"Now. We're starting again. This time I want youse to ... "

"Can *I* play, mister?"

They all turned round. There was a girl there, all got up in the proper kit. She looked sturdy and had a round, rosy face and her black hair was tied back in a pony tail. And she was smiling, hopefully. "Tried other teams, yer see, but they won't have me."

The wingy studied her. "D'yer know the game? Played before?"

"Yes. I'm good at it. Played wing-forward for Everton."

The Cats team fell about and Mr Oliver said, "Yer coddin' me, aren't yer?"

"No, I'm not." The girl frowned. "Should of said Everton Lane. Was where we was living before we moved to Joseph Terrace. Sorry ... "

"That's all right, luv. But d'yer not want ter play for Joseph's?"

She shook her head.

"Well ... what do youse think?" The wingy put it to the team.

The Nabber stopped chewing to say, "We don't want girls playin'. They're no good at it."

"What about it, Rocky?" asked the wingy.

Rocky considered the matter. They needed more players. "We don't know what she's like. Give her a chance. If she can play – she can come on the team."

And she *could* play. She got the ball and took it straight down to the goal and right through Beady's defence. The Cats stood in silence while Beady went to get it.

"Well," said Mr Oliver. "Yer have ter give it to her. She can play all right. What's yer name?"

"Bobbie," she said, panting. And seeing a look of disbelief on the Cats' faces she added, "Me real name's Roberta. But I don't like it, see? So I'm Bobbie. Bobbie Sissley."

The Cats gang watched Bobbie Sissley walking away with the wingy through the park, talking enthusiastically about soccer.

"Come on, wacks," said Rocky and they followed him down to the lake that rippled under a cold wind. The trees were leafless and black against the sky and the big houses round the park, harassed by time and neglect and vandals, looked blind and broken. Sea-birds swooped down for scraps of bread and pram-pushing mothers went by at the speed of knots and the ducks paddled round, impervious to cold but keeping themselves aloof from the Cats, and especially Suzie, who was throwing stones at them.

"She can't be the Sissler," Rocky said, after a lot of thought.

"Could be," said Beady. "You seen these women athletes?"

"Chick an' Spadge didn't say the Sissler was a girl."

"Same name, in't it, but?" said the Nabber.

"Tell yer what, Billy, yer could ask round Joseph's. See what yer come up with."

"Do me best," said Billy and made a note of it, but he was reluctant to ask too many questions round Joseph's.

"No way she's comin' on the team if she's the Sissler. No way," the Nabber said, firmly.

"That'll be up to *me*," retorted Rocky. "And maybe Billy."

"What's *he* got ter do with it? Can't walk proper, never mind run."

"He can organize a match and you couldn't even organize that man that would sell yer ... "

"Wasn't my fault – told yer that – he moved on ... "

"What yer mean moved on? Yer just a big mouth – s'like looking into the Mersey Tunnel when you open yer mouth!"

Rocky and the Nabber were really worked up and squaring up for a fight.

"Knock it off, wacks," said Beady, quietly. "Can't see her being the Sissler, but we'll find out."

"Ah, come on!" Rocky hunched his shoulders against the cold and started walking towards Princes

Boulevard, his anger and irritation about the team's poor showing and the problem of the Sissler subsiding as he began to make plans. "Listen," he said, "I've got an idea – fer makin' a lot of money. Tell yer about it. This afternoon. The hideout."

The Cats didn't respond immediately to this, then Billy said, "Sorry, Rocky. My Grandad's comin' today."

"Goin' ter the match with me dad," said the Nabber.

"Have to go to Chinese Centre to practise flute," said Little Chan.

"Goin' to me auntie's with me mam," Beady said.

Rocky's anger erupted again. "Ter yer auntie's? With yer mam? Catch me goin' ter me auntie's with me mam!"

"Yer haven't got a auntie, have yer?"

"Yes, I have. Got a auntie Chrissie. Yer a lot of characters," he concluded. "What about ternight, den? Six – at the hideout?"

"Well, me dad's gorra video, but I could watch it termorrow," the Nabber conceded.

Mrs Flanagan was ensconced in her chair by the electric fire, immersed in one of her romances. At the table Suzie was absorbed in colouring in the pictures in Rocky's *Eagle* – the one with the Alien in it – among the plates they'd had their fish fingers and peas off and the empty mugs and the bottle of milk and the bottle of tomato sauce and the packet of sliced bread. Apart from the ticking and occasional hiccuping of the alarm clock, the silence was awful. And so was the deserted Square. Rocky glared out at it. Everybody he knew had gone somewhere. He was the only one with nothing to do. Not until he could get the Cats together and make plans. The afternoon stretched blankly before him. Could go to the Youth Club, he thought. He'd seen a notice outside the Baptist Church saying they had a session that afternoon. But he hadn't any money for subs – apart from the twenty – and anyway he'd been thrown out for fighting last time he'd been there, and then he'd got the Cats to tramp round on the flat roof of the Church Hall while they were singing hymns inside to get his own back. But if he *could* join again he would be able to go to their Christmas party and take Suzie with him. He'd been to one of their Christmas parties and it was good – plenty to eat and presents. But you had to have your subs.

In his frustration, he started kicking at the skirting-board. His mother looked up.

"Stop doin' that. Yer'll have a hole in it. Get yerself out."

"Nowhere to go, but."

"Well sit yerself down and shut up."

"Could go ter the youth club if yer'd give me some money."

"There's no money fer that! Put the telly on if yer've nothin' else to do!" And she went back to her romance.

Rocky switched on the telly and slumped on to

the sofa beside Suzie. He looked at the comic she was colouring.

"What yer given him a pink head for – the Alien?" he asked.

Suzie looked at him. "Got a pink head," she said, flatly.

Rocky let it go at that. You couldn't argue with Suzie. He made his mind up. He would try the Youth Club again. Yer never knew. They might have forgotten what he did. Couldn't change the twenty there, but he might get in free. He went out quietly without Suzie or his mother noticing. It was daylight – and he didn't think the terrorist would attack him in daylight, but he kept a sharp watch out for him.

The Church Hall was crowded, with the table tennis and the darts and the popmobility going. Rocky pushed his way through to where Betty Mulloney, who lived near Rocky, was serving tea.

"Hi, Betty," he said, being very friendly, "give us a cup. Forgot me money, but I'll pay yer next week … "

"Yer not a member," said Betty, decisively. "And Mr Cooper said yer couldn't come back."

"What for but?"

"Yer know what for."

"Wur's Mr Cooper?"

"He's not here. It's Mr Ferndean now."

"The management's changed den, has it?" asked Rocky, spotting a loop-hole. "Wur's Mr Ferndean den?"

"I'll take yer."

He followed Betty Mulloney over to where a young man in a pink sweater was refereeing the table tennis. Rocky summed him up while Betty Mulloney was saying, "This is Rocky O'Rourke. He's from the Square. Mr Cooper said he couldn't come back because he only comes for the Christmas party and he had a fight last time he come."

"You watch it, Betty Mulloney," hissed Rocky.

"Now then, Rocky. No need for that. And we're all entitled to make a few mistakes, Betty," said Mr Ferndean.

"But yer don't *know* him ... " began Betty Mulloney.

"That's all right, Betty. Now, Rocky" – Mr Ferndean smiled at Rocky and Rocky immediately had visions of him and Suzie at the Christmas party – "why do you want to come back to the club?"

You could have spread Rocky's innocence on bread, like honey. "Well, mister, yer see, it's nice and warm and friendly and me mam's out a lot and ... "

"But you'll behave yourself?"

"Honest. But yer see I haven't got der money for the subs or the tea this week, but ... "

"That's what he always says," put in Betty Mulloney.

"You can have this week free *and* a cup of tea. Next week, you'll have to pay. Now what's your interest? Darts? Table tennis?"

Rocky reflected on which was the least boring.

"I'll play darts," he said.

"All right. Now get your tea."

Rocky was on his best behaviour. He only knocked over the jug of milk when Betty Mulloney reluctantly gave him his tea and biscuit, tripped up one of the table-tennis players – accidentally – and nudged a member of the other darts team when he was about to throw. Apart from that, nobody would have known that Rocky O'Rourke was around. At four o'clock he went into the darkening October night with the rest, he had a bit of a punch-up with the table-tennis player he'd tripped up and ran off home certain he had a good thing going there. All he had to do, he reflected, was to get his subs somehow. And he could get them when he sold the gear from the Rialto, or changed the twenty.

At six o'clock, silent and unobtrusive as a shadow and even more cautious than usual, but with his mind seething with ideas, he crept down the steps to the hideout and gave the Cats' special knock before going in.

"Hi, wacks!" he said and joined the gang round the card table.

"This big plan," said the Nabber. "Better be a good one after what I've give up ter hear about it."

"It's good. Listen. This is it. Tomorrow night we're doin' the Rialto – takin' all the gear out – tomorrow night."

The Cats thought about it, then Beady said, "What about the Sissler?"

"Yer mean that girl?" asked the Nabber, scornfully.

"I don't think she's the Sissler," said Billy.

"Same name."

"Doesn't matter *who* the Sissler is, see?" said Rocky. "Thing is ter get the loot."

"But it's stolen stuff, Rocky," said Billy.

"We didn't steal it but, skin. Once it's been stole once, can't be stole again, can it? Doesn't belong to nobody now."

Billy thought there was something wrong with this, but didn't want to disagree.

"It's on then," said Rocky. "And we stash all the gear in here."

"What about the transport?" The Nabber sat back with the air of somebody who knew what he was talking about. "Yer've got ter have transport for that lot."

"Got it all worked out. We have ter have a Guy Fawkes. If we're doin' the Rialto, we have ter have a Guy Fawkes."

"A Guy Fawkes? What's a Guy Fawkes ter do with it? What's he on about now?" asked the Nabber, derisively. "First it's the mugger, then it's the Alien, now it's a Guy Fawkes!"

Rocky leaned forward impressively. "Because it's nearly Guy Fawkes' night, in't it? And if we're wheeling a guy round in something with the loot under him nobody's goin' ter think nothin' about it. It's a cover, see?"

"He's right, man," said Beady.

"It sounds ingenious," Little Chan said.

"Could make some money on the side," the

Nabber suggested.

"And then we sell the loot to that woman you know in the Buildings," said Rocky.

The Nabber pushed his hat back. "Oh her – but yer know … "

"But how do we make the guy?" asked Billy, hoping they wouldn't be able to and the whole thing would be called off. "Take a lot of time ter make a guy."

"We're not makin' one. One of *us*'ll be the guy. I'll get Suzie's crayons ter do the face up and a blanket ter put over him and he can wear the Nabber's hat."

"Who'll it be?" asked Beady.

"It's a sittin' down job. Better be Billy," said the Nabber.

"No – Billy keeps dowse like always. He knows how ter do it and he can hoot like a owl ter warn us if anybody's comin'. It'll have ter be Little Chan. And bring yer torch, Chan. Mine's not very good and that creep in Lewis's took my new batteries off me."

"My father," began Little Chan, but Rocky broke in. "*He* won't know nothin' about it. And it'll just take half an hour."

"Yer still need transport," the Nabber insisted. "Yer've got ter have somethin' ter put the guy and the gear in."

"Leave it ter me," said Rocky. "Got it all worked out."

"Ellen! Hi, Ellen!"

98

After a minute or two, the upstairs window was pushed open and Ellen looked out, her blonde hair illuminated in the light from the room behind her.

"Who's it?"

"S'me – Rocky."

"What's up then? Yer mam out again?"

"No, Ellen. It's the pram. Can I borrow yer pram? Tomorrow night?"

Ellen hesitated. "What yer want me pram for?" she asked, suspiciously.

"It's Guy Fawkes. Ter put the guy in, see? Only want it a hour."

"Well, I don't know, Rocky ... "

"But yer take Trevor in about five, don't yer? Would only want it till six and yer'll not be needin' it."

"Not that, Rocky," said Ellen. "See, if somethin' happened to it – well, I can't get another one."

"Nothin'll happen to it – honest!" Rocky shouted up.

"Well, I don't know ... "

The door of number 4 St Catherine's Square was flung open and a woman stepped out on to the pavement. "Will youse stop yer noise?" she shouted. "Youse always at it! There's no peace here with youse lot!"

Ellen shouted back immediately, "Who d'yer think yer talkin' to? And what yer on about? I can hear you lot through the wall all night!"

"That's right," Rocky put in, "all night!" Though

he'd never heard them.

"I'll be on to the landlord about yer – he'll throw yer out!"

"Try it on! My rent's never behind!"

"And put a trap on yer moey!" was Rocky's final contribution to the conversation.

The woman from number 4 went inside and slammed the door.

"Her complain about *me*? I'll complain about *her*! The cheek! And just because of Trevor!"

"Trevor? What's Trevor done?" Rocky shouted back, puzzled.

"Got born, didn't he?"

Rocky pushed a hand through his hair desperately. "Look, Ellen, *can* I have the pram? It'll be all right."

Ellen took some time to subside and think about it. "Yer puttin' a guy in it?"

"Yes."

"Wur yer goin' with it but?"

"Just along Prinney Boulevard. Just for a hour."

"All right well. But mind, Rocky, if yer break it up … "

"Won't, Ellen. Honest."

"All right. After I take Trevor in."

It was half past five and already dark when the Cats started along Princes Boulevard to the Rialto. Rocky pushed the pram in which Little Chan sat, a moustache painted on his face and the Nabber's camouflage hat eclipsing him. Nabber and Beady walked alongside and Billy pedalled anxiously behind. He didn't like it and he wished Rocky wouldn't get such ideas. He didn't want to go near the Rialto and he didn't want to go near Joseph Terrace after dark. Little Chan felt the same and also hoped that Rocky wouldn't upset the pram, which was wobbling a lot.

"Yer not doing it proper," Rocky panted. "Yer not askin' for pennies. The cover's no good if yer don't … "

"I'm goin' off this," said the Nabber.

"Penny for the guy, missus," said Beady to a passer-by.

"Go on, Nabber!" hissed Rocky.

"Hi – give's a penny for the guy," the Nabber demanded, threateningly.

They turned into Joseph Terrace. "Youse can shut up now," whispered Rocky. "And watch out."

There were no tiddlers about and no sign of Chick's Lot. They passed the pub which was still closed and turned into the dark lane behind the Rialto. It was *very* dark – black. They couldn't see each other and only the squeaking wheel on the pram helped them to stay together. Then Rocky stopped, "This is it," he whispered. "Billy, keep dowse and hoot if anybody comes. I'll get in first. Beady and Nabber – you follow."

It was very quiet when the three of them had gone into the Rialto and the light of the torch had disappeared.

"Don't like this, Billy," whispered Little Chan

from under the Nabber's hat.

Billy didn't answer, but he was wishing he was home in the flat in St Catherine's with his mother and brother. Rocky was a good skin, but he did take risks.

"You keepin' dowse, Billy? Anybody about?"

"I'll go down to the end of the lane – see what's goin' on," and Billy cycled away.

Little Chan sat very still. What would he do, he wondered, if Billy started hooting like an owl? He couldn't see himself running home in the Nabber's hat with a moustache painted on his face!

The light from the torch slithered over the car radios and the other loot.

"This is it," Rocky said, quietly, but his voice still echoed in the emptiness. It was very cold and still and threatening, and even the Nabber felt he had to speak in a whisper.

"Got ter give it to the Sissler," he said. "If he took this lot, he's into it, in't he?"

"Can't take all of it," said Beady. "Them radios – we'll never unload them."

"That box of ciggies – I can get rid of them – straight off," said the Nabber. "And them shirts."

"There's a box of desert-wellies can go – and I might get a pair out of them. Come on, then, Beady. You go out first and we'll pass the stuff to yer … "

"What's that on the wall?" the Nabber asked, suddenly.

Rocky shone the torch. "The Sissler – he wrote it."

"Further up but."

"Me and Suzie did that."

"Dead give away, in't it?" said the Nabber.

Billy came back fast. "They're there. Chick's Lot. In the Terrace. On motor bikes."

Little Chan sank further down into the pram, just as Beady's voice came from the broken window – "We're comin' out."

"Chick and Spadge – down there," Billy whispered.

Then Rocky's voice said, "Yer should of hooted, Billy. They comin' down here?"

"Don't think so."

"We'll take the risk. Go and check again, Billy. Yer can hoot if it's all right."

Billy went off again, puzzled. He'd always thought he had to hoot if there was danger, not if there wasn't.

They loaded up the stuff, and Little Chan was a lot higher up in the pram than he had been. Then Billy hooted from the end of the lane and they started pushing. They went back faster than they came and they didn't ask for pennies.

"Rocky, it's dangerous," Billy panted as he cycled alongside. "Not just Chick and Spadge – it's stolen stuff – the scuffers can get yer for stolen stuff – I told yer … "

"Yer worry too much, skin," said Rocky. "I've

got it all worked out. The scuffers'll never know."

They got the stuff into the hideout and stowed it away in cupboards and corners. And Rocky got himself a pair of desert-wellies that fitted. He pranced round in the candlelight. "Hi!" he shouted. "Look at dese! Dese is just right!"

The Cats watched him, uncertainly, and the Nabber said, "Just the things ter get yer done. They're hot."

"I'll get them muckied up a bit. Nobody'll notice them. And we'll get a lot for all this stuff. And we did it, didn't we?" Rocky said, triumphantly. "We did the Sissler! And how much did we get for the guy?"

"Twenty-five pence," said the Nabber.

"Right. We'll get some chips – come on!"

CHAPTER

10

A BIT later, Rocky pushed the pram on to the pavement outside number 3 and stopped to examine the motor bike parked by the kerb. It was big and powerful, with a lot of badges on the front. Looks like an armoured car, he thought. Must be Ellen-from-upstairs' boyfriend's. He must have money. Maybe be could get a ride on it. He shouted up at Ellen's window, "Hi – Ellen!"

After a minute, the curtains parted, the window was pushed open and Ellen looked out. "Who's it?"

"Me. Brought the pram back."

"Thanks, luv. Put it in the passage."

"Hi, Ellen – whose is the bike?"

"What? Don't know." And the window was pulled down. Then it was pushed up again. "Yer'll put the brake on? On the pram?"

"Course I will!"

"Thanks, luv."

More thoughtfully, Rocky took another look at the motor bike. It could mean that his brother Joey was back. He pushed Ellen's pram into the passage of number 3 and went into the living-room. The telly was on, the electric fire going full blast, and there was Joey, sitting in his mother's chair, feet on a stool, cigarette in his hand and a paper in front of his face. Joey's bike, Rocky thought and slammed the door behind him deliberately and defiantly.

Joey looked up. "Rocky! Hello dur, skin! How's things?"

Rocky flopped on to the sofa where Suzie was huddled into a corner and picked up one of his comics. His mother looked round indignantly from the gas stove, brandishing the kettle. "Yer got nothin' ter say ter yer brother when he's just back from the Antarctic?" she demanded.

"Not the Antarctic, mam. Was Canada," said Joey.

"Well, Canada. You said there was ice and snow, but."

"What's it like?" asked Rocky.

"He says it's smashin'!" said Mrs Flanagan, enthusiastically.

"What's he come back for then?" asked Rocky.

"I'll leather yer! It's his home, in't it? He's got a right ter come back!"

"S'all right, mam. Don't get worked up." And Joey retired behind his newspaper.

Rocky's contempt for Joey welled up. He remembered when he'd tried to save Joey from Jim Simpson, going into the graveyard by the Cathedral where Joey was hiding from Jim Simpson and then down to the snack bar at Pier Head to find the man Joey said would take him off on his boat to safety. And now Joey was back, acting as if it had never happened – as if he'd never threatened Flanagan and made his mam give him money. Anyway, Joey had never got the amount of loot together that Rocky had in the hideout!

"How long yer been in Birkenhead?" he asked, suddenly.

Joey looked over the newspaper at him. "What yer mean?"

"Yer card was posted in Birkenhead – 'bout two weeks ago. Do it by remote control, did yer?"

Joey grinned. "He's with it, is our Rocky."

"Two weeks? Yer haven't been back two weeks, Joey, and never come home!" said Mrs Flanagan, dismayed.

"Couldn't tell yer, mam. Had some business ter do, see? Couldn't come home till it was settled."

"Oh, business. Well, that's different," said Mrs Flanagan and handed Joey a cup of tea and then went to Rocky, a plastic carrier bag and her purse in her hand. "Rocky," she said, confidentially, "we'll have somethin' nice for the tea now Joey's back. Will yer go down to Pa Richardson's?"

Rocky hesitated, thinking about the Steps in the darkness and the terrorist. But he could go the long way round through St Catherine's Buildings and down Joseph Terrace. It would be worth risking Chick's Lot and the tiddlers if he could make a good bargain with his mother.

"What yer mean 'nice'?" he asked.

"Well, we could have pizzas and a tin of beans and yer could get some frozen chips. Look, here's two pounds. And get a sliced loaf as well."

"Can I get some cakes?"

"If there's any money left, yer can."

"There won't be, but."

"Well, here's another fifty pence. Don't go wanderin' off, mind – come straight back. And get yourself off or he'll be closed. And what's them on your feet?"

"Me desert-wellies."

"They're different. Let's see them."

Reluctantly, Rocky stuck his feet out.

"Wur'd yer get *them*?"

"Had ter get them somewhere – *you* wouldn't get me any ... "

"But them's new!"

"Der not. Der *nearly* new, see. Got them for fifty pence. Jumble sale at the Youth Club."

"Yer not in the Youth Club."

"Don't have ter be. Not for the jumble. Yer can just walk in." Rocky's imagination took over. "Yer should have gone, mam. There was all sorts, like sweaters and cardies and coats – everything. All cheap."

Mrs Flanagan's suspicions increased. "*I* didn't see no notices."

"Dey was all over."

"I wus always gettin' things cheap from jumble sales," said Joey, meaningfully, grinning behind his newspaper.

Rocky glared at him with angry, tiger-yellow eyes, then turned back to his mother, talking fast to take her mind off the desert-wellies. "Listen, but. I'm joinin' the Youth Club again, see, and I'll want me subs and ... "

"I've got no money for subs."

"Yer've got the money for pizzas for him!"

"Shut yer mouth or I'll shut it for yer!" shouted Mrs Flanagan, feeling she was caught up in something she didn't understand – and didn't want to.

"I'll give yer the subs," said Joey, putting his hand in his pocket.

Rocky was tempted – a bit of cash always came in useful. But then he decided he wasn't having any handouts from Joey. "Yer can keep yer money," he retorted.

"Yer an ungrateful little – " shouted Mrs Flanagan.

Joey shrugged. "Doesn't matter, mam. Better in my pocket than his." And he went back to his newspaper.

"Get yerself off," said Mrs Flanagan.

Rocky gave a quick look at Suzie, but she didn't seem to have heard anything – she was just staring obsessively at Joey.

As he looked round the Square, Rocky's feelings were in a turmoil. He'd admired Joey so much and wanted to be like him – a big criminal, lots of money, but Joey had just been lying to him. Made a fool of him. And now he was back, sponging off their mam again – *and* with that big bike. Yer couldn't buy one of *them* for peanuts! Rocky gave the bike a contemptuous look and made for the Steps. But then a car turned into the Square and came slowly and menacingly towards him, its headlights dazzling him. As it slid to a stop beside him, he stepped backwards, apprehensive, wondering whether to run. Then the headlights were dimmed and a man inside said, "Wur yer off to, lad?"

Rocky could only just make out the face in the car and he relaxed – it wasn't the terrorist – and anyway he knew a jack when he met one, and the voice of a policeman over the crackling car radio confirmed it.

"What's it ter do with you?"

"None of that now. Just answer the question."

Rocky was about to give him a bit of lip when he thought of the loot stashed in the hideout just a few yards away. Maybe the jack had had word about it – maybe, even if he hadn't heard, he'd start asking questions if Rocky got stroppy with him. Rocky put on a more subdued manner.

"Goin' down the lanney – ter the shop. For me mam, see."

The plain-clothes detective was looking at him too carefully for Rocky's peace of mind. Was it the gear in the hideout? Or maybe it was Joey – maybe Joey had …

"What's yer name, lad?"

"Rocky. Rocky O'Rourke. I live over there … " It made him sweat more than lifting the gear from the Rialto.

The car radio crackled again. " … all patrols – theft from the person – Hardman Street … "

The jack went on, looking at him, "Where's over there?"

"Number 3."

"Where the bike is?"

Rocky was sweating even more – the jack could start asking about Joey yet.

"That's right. The bike's the feller's upstairs – not mine."

"Didn't think it was yours. Watch out then, Rocky, and don't get into anything – " and he took the car through a U-turn and back to Princes Boulevard. In relief and anger, Rocky made several vulgar gestures at its retreating rear lights.

Pa Richardson saw Rocky come into his shop and a look of caution came over his long, cavernous face. He was always suspicious of Rocky and the Cats. He sniffed, put a bag of sugar on the counter and said, "That's thirty-four, Mrs Baines. Anything else? Just a minute." And he bumbled over to the door like an underfed bee with a cold and turned the notice in the window from "Open" to "Closed". "Half of marg, was it?"

The white neon lighting, cold as the small, stuffy shop with its smells of cheese and detergents and slightly rancid bacon, cast shadows into every hollow of his face.

"Closing early, are yer?" asked Mrs Baines.

"Safety first. Wouldn't like ter tell yer what it cost me ter have them wire frames put on the window. And I had ter pay VAT."

"But the shop's not been done?"

"Cheeky young – sniff – nobody," said Pa

Richardson, looking hard at Rocky, "come in and wanted – sniff – fifty pounds and he'd see I wasn't done. Told him I'd – sniff – clip his ear for him. I'm thinkin' of retirin' and sellin' up."

Rocky was listening to all this with interest, but he took the opportunity of Pa Richardson being engaged in conversation to have a wander round the shop.

"But what would we do without yer?" Mrs Baines pushed her groceries into her shopping bag.

"Go ter Tesco, wouldn't yer? That the lot? That's four pounds ninety four. It's a desert round here – sniff. Will yer shut the door after yer – sniff – and what *you* after?" he asked Rocky. "If it's that box of chocolates yer've just picked up, bring it – sniff – over here."

Rocky put the chocolates back on the shelf and stalked angrily to the counter. "Was just lookin' at it."

"Oh – sniff – lookin's free," said Pa Richardson. "But the chocolates isn't. Now what d'yer want?"

Rocky glared at him. Pa Richardson had a disconcerting manner that suggested that he knew a lot more than he would tell. "A sliced loaf, big tin of beans and four pizzas – the small ones. If der's no small ones, two big ones."

Pa Richardson moved slowly round, picking up the items and putting them carefully on the counter. Rocky watched him, then asked, pretending to be casual, "Wus he called Sissley – the one that wanted the fifty?"

"Called what? Didn't ask him. Cleared him off. That all?"

"How long yer had them cakes in?" Rocky asked, indicating a box on the counter.

Pa Richardson paused, calculating. "Fresh this mornin'."

"How much?"

"Seven pence each."

"Give yer five pence each for four."

"Yer on." Pa Richardson put four cakes into a paper bag and handed them over. "Yer brother must be back. Let him out, did they?"

"What yer mean out? He's been away – ter Canada," Rocky retorted, indignantly.

"Canada? That's a new name for Walton Jail. And that's a pound for the pizzas, thirty for the loaf, twenty-five for the beans and twenty for the cakes – that's one seventy-five."

Rocky thought desperately and then decided to take the risk. He got out the twenty pound note and dropped it, casually, on the counter. Pa Richardson didn't pick it up. He just looked at it, then he said, "Don't see many of – sniff – them. Don't take them. Run away with me change. Can't keep on – sniff – goin' down to the bank. That all yer've got?"

Angrily, Rocky dropped his mother's two pounds on the counter. "Will changin' *them* break yer?" and as Pa Richardson turned away to the till, he picked up another cake and dropped it into the plastic bag. Then he smiled at Pa Richardson as he took his change. "Thanks, Mr Richardson," he said.

Pa Richardson frowned suspiciously at such politeness. "Who's this Sissley – sniff – one of Joseph's lot? Yer – sniff – in with them? That where the – sniff – twenty pounds come from?"

"None of your business," said Rocky, angry again. "But if yer have ter know, it's our Joey's."

"That – sniff – explains it. Got it in Canada, did he?"

"Yes! He did!"

"That's news. Didn't know they had them – sniff – out there."

"None of your business where he got it from anyway!"

"Might be of interest – sniff – to them lot at Larkspur police station," said Pa Richardson, thoughtfully.

"What yer mean? What yer sayin' about our Joey? I'll tell me mam ... "

"Could be – sniff – a good idea."

That made Rocky a bit worried. Things got around. He started for the door, but when he was out of the shop, he turned round and shouted, "Yer'll trip over yer nose yet!" And he paused for a moment to enjoy the sight of Pa Richardson's angry face in the shop doorway before he went off at a run, fishing the extra cake out of the bag and munching it as he went. Done him, he thought, triumphantly. Done him!

He was so elated and triumphant that he forgot to go back the long way round and started running up the Steps. But then he remembered and stopped and looked upwards. A skeletal figure, outlined by the light from the street lamp, stood above him. Rocky didn't hesitate. He turned to run back, but two arms encircled him, tight bands over his chest, lifting him off his feet. He dropped the groceries and squirmed like a fish on a hook until a hoarse voice that he recognized said, "Keep still, yer little bastard, and keep quiet – or I'll break yer neck!"

Rocky went still – and silent.

The voice, close to his ear – he could feel the man's breath on his face – said, "That man yer helped the other night – where'd he go?"

"Don't know, mister," Rocky gasped. "Honest."

"Yer'd better know."

"Got a taxi – just went off."

He was swung round and a fist caught him across the face, half-stunning him and his legs gave way and he fell.

"Gerrup, will yer!"

As the man slapped him, Rocky would have told him anything – even the phone number he had, if he could have remembered it – just to stop the man beating him up. "Listen, mister," he shouted, "it's in me pocket – only thing I got from him … "

Then a high, thin voice called from down the Steps, "Leave that boy alone! I'll have the police on ter yer!" And he was lying on the Steps and the man had gone and he heard the high voice protesting, "He shoved me out of the way – I'll have him for it. I'll … "

Rocky staggered to his feet and made out the old

woman in the red woolly cap leaning against the wall, but he couldn't help her then.

Mrs Flanagan was combing her hair in front of the mirror on the mantelpiece and Joey was having a doze in the chair and Suzie was behind the sofa when Rocky came in. His mother didn't turn round, but put down the comb and picked up her lipstick.

"Yer've taken yer time," she said. "Have yer got the things? Don't make a noise – yer'll wake him. And he needs his rest after all that travelling about."

Rocky dropped on to the sofa. The ceiling was swinging round above his head, so he closed his eyes.

"Here, what's up with yer? What yer doin'?" he heard his mother say.

"Fell down," he muttered.

"Fell? What d'yer mean fell?" His mother came to look at him. "Yer'd have ter fall down off the Buildings ter look like that! And where's the pizzas?"

"Dropped them." Rocky tasted blood in his mouth.

"*Dropped* them? Dropped them *wur*?"

Joey woke up and came to look at Rocky. "He's out," he said. "He's right out!"

CHAPTER

11

WHEN Rocky came round, Ellen-from-upstairs was bending over him, wiping his face with a wet cloth that smelt strongly of Trevor and he could see Joey behind her and he could hear his mother having hysterics somewhere.

"He's all right, Mrs Flanagan. He's all right. Yer all right, luv?" Ellen, her long hair hanging over her face, smiled down at him.

Rocky struggled to sit up. "All right," he muttered, but the pain in his arm was awful and he fell back again.

His mother stopped having hysterics and came to look at him.

"Yer've been fightin'," she said, accusingly.

"Haven't."

"We'd better have the doctor. Go on, our Joey. On yer bike. Get the ... "

"Don't want him," said Rocky. He closed his eyes. His face was throbbing down one side. "Think I've got a tooth loose."

"What's that? What yer say, luv?" asked his mother.

"Get him a cup of tea, Mrs Flanagan," said Ellen-from-upstairs. "Plenty of sugar. That's what yer give fer shock."

"Fer shock? Well, it's me that needs it!" She went to fill the kettle. "Ellen, luv," she said over her shoulder, "will yer see if yer can find Mr Oliver? He'll know what ter do ... "

Rocky opened his eyes again. He seemed to be by himself now, but then Joey's face looked down at him. "Rocky," he whispered urgently, "yer was done, wasn't yer? Beaten up? Was it Jim Simpson's lot? Wus dey after me? Yer didn't say I was back, did yer? Rocky? Did yer?"

Same old Joey, Rocky thought. Thinks he's the centre of the universe and he's scared stiff all the time.

But then Mr Oliver and Ellen were there and Joey had merged into the background.

"What's all this then, lad?" Mr Oliver asked.

"Fell down. On the Steps."

"Yer must of gone from top ter bottom. Yer've gashed yer lip. Broken anything? Here, let's have a look."

Rocky winced as he touched his arm.

"That's it. Sprained yer arm. Nothin' broken. Yer better have it in a sling. Stay put and I'll get some bandage. Mrs Flanagan, he'll need a cold, wet towel on his face over that cut. How come yer did all this damage just falling down the Steps?"

Rocky sensed Mr Oliver's suspicion and said quickly, "Just slipped, yer know like."

"It's not his shoes, but," said his mother, on the

defensive. "He's got a new pair of them."

"Bought them for him with yer twenty pounds?" asked Mr Oliver.

Mrs Flanagan was shocked. "Twenty pounds? What twenty pounds? Wur would *I* get twenty pounds? He got them in the jumble sale for fifty pence." Then a sudden thought struck her. "Where'd yer get the fifty pence from but? Yer was on at me about money for subs, but if yer had fifty pence … "

"Mr Oliver," said Rocky, quickly, "I dropped the groceries on the Steps. Would yer get them for me mam?"

Mr Oliver got slowly to his feet. "Right, Rocky. I'll get them. That all yer got ter say?" he asked, significantly.

"Yes, Mr Oliver." And Rocky started drinking the tea his mother had brought him.

"Wur's Joey?"

The ceiling had stopped turning round and Rocky felt better.

Mrs Flanagan dropped into her chair. "He's gone. Had ter see somebody. I don't know," she sobbed. "Nothin' goes right. And we was goin' ter have a nice tea!"

"How much yer give him?"

"*Give* him? What yer mean give him?" Mrs Flanagan sobbed indignantly, then she said, "Well, I give him a couple of pounds. He's got money comin' to him, but he hasn't got it yet."

Knew he'd get something, Rocky thought.

"Now you have a nice sleep and I'll wake yer up fer yer tea when it's ready."

Rocky closed his eyes and he did fall asleep – he couldn't help it, but he had a terrible dream of being chased by the terrorist. It was in Chan's chippy and Mrs Chan was standing watching and Little Chan was playing his flute and the terrorist was chasing him round the counter, but his feet were like lead and he wasn't moving at all and the terrorist got him and was pushing his head down into the pan of boiling fat. Rocky wakened up then, sweating and shouting. Suzie had got up from behind the sofa where she'd been hiding and was looking at him, her eyes wide.

"Hurt," she said. "Hurt, Rocky."

"Wur yer been, tatty-'ead?" he asked, relieved to find himself at home.

"Been here. Hurt, Rocky."

Mrs Flanagan looked down at him. "What yer yellin' for? Yer all right, Rocky?" But then there was a smell of burning and she dashed back to the cooker. Rocky closed his eyes, trying to shut out the memory of that hoarse voice.

He heard Suzie whisper, "Dead. Dead, Rocky."

"I'm not dead, tatty-'ead. Told yer. If yer face isn't covered with a sheet yer not dead!"

Suzie smiled. "Not dead, Rocky."

From the cooker came the sound of Mrs Flanagan scraping pieces off the pizzas.

"Burnt," said Suzie, with satisfaction. And added,

"*He's* gone. On bike." And she started racing about the room making a noise like a motor bike.

Mrs Flanagan turned round, brandishing a knife. "Will yer give that up, Suzie Flanagan, or I'll batter yer!"

Suzie stopped and crept up to Rocky. He propped himself up on his good arm and said, confidentially, "Look, Suzie, der's some cakes in that bag on the table. Yer can get us one each. And yer can get me comics off me bed. Right den?"

He didn't go to school next day. He lay on the sofa and read his comics and in the afternoon Mr Oliver came in to see how he was, but he didn't say much, though he looked as though he wanted to say something. Then he said, "When yer better, Rocky, we'll have a talk," and went away. Ellen-from-upstairs brought him a bag of sweets and his mother went out for some shopping. While she was away, the afternoon darkened and Rocky lay watching the window, thinking that the terrorist might peer through at any time. And he thought of the old woman in the red woolly hat – she'd saved him from the terrorist. She might be crazy, but she'd saved him. Have ter thank her, he thought.

His mother came back, followed by Suzie, and switched on the light. Rocky felt more vulnerable than ever, lying there in front of the window.

"Mam, will yer close the curtains?" he asked.

Mrs Flanagan pulled them together and fastened them with the pin and Rocky felt safer. His mother began combing her hair frantically in front of the mirror above the fireplace and putting on lipstick.

"I've got yer some crisps and some Coke and der's sausages and a tin of beans fer yer tea. Yer can manage them, can't yer?"

"Yer not goin' out? Yer not leavin' me?" said Rocky, indignantly.

"Yer'll be all right. I'm just goin' ter see yer auntie Chrissie. I'll not be long. And yer can give *her* her tea," she said, not looking at Suzie.

"Yer leavin' me ter go ter auntie Chrissie's when I'm not well?"

"Yer not disabled."

"Typical! It's typical!"

"What yer mean typical? She's expectin' me is Chrissie and I'll not be long and yer can manage … Yer can just lie there and watch the telly."

As she switched it on there was a cautious knocking at the door. Mrs Flanagan froze. "Who's that?" she shouted and a voice outside said, "Rocky? Yer comin' out, Rocky?"

"That's Beady," said Rocky, happily. "Come on in, Beady!"

The door opened and all the Cats came in, standing close to the door and looking anxiously from Rocky to Mrs Flanagan.

"What do you lot want?" she asked.

"They've come ter see *me*," said Rocky. "They'll not do any harm and you're goin' out."

Mrs Flanagan considered the matter, then she said, "Well, they haven't got to touch the telly, mind. Suzie knows how ter change the channels. And yer can give them those Cokes and crisps and I want all of youse out of here before I come back!"

The door slammed behind her, the television flickered and talked and the Cats stood about, embarrassed, looking round the place. They'd never been in Rocky's home before. Billy thought it was the barest room he'd seen – nothing like the comfortable sitting-room at home. And the Nabber just thought it looked like a junk shop and no sign of a video or a music centre like his dad had.

It was the Nabber who spoke first. Taking in Rocky's bruised face and swollen lip, he said, complimentarily, "Yer don't look bad for a bull-dog."

"Do yer fer that when me arm's better!"

"Think yer'd broke yer neck!"

"Those steps are dangerous," said Little Chan.

"Go on! He's been up and down them enough! What really happened? Was the mugger again, wasn't it?"

"How d'yer know that?" asked Rocky.

"Always the mugger, in't it?"

Rocky didn't answer. The Nabber could talk all he liked – he didn't know the danger.

There was another awkward silence, then Rocky said, "What yer all standin' round like road-workers for?" and the gang relaxed and sat down on the floor.

"Where's the refreshments?" asked the Nabber.

"There's the crisps and Coke. Suzie can get them.

And there's sausages and beans. Only we'll have ter cook them. We can have a party." Rocky became enthusiastic and sat up, wincing as he put his weight on his arm – but he'd never had a party at home before.

The Nabber investigated. "There's six sausages," he concluded. "That's one each and about half a dozen beans. This is the Ritz!"

"Belt up, Nabber! One of youse'll have ter fry the sausages, but yer have ter watch the cooker or it flares up. Suzie, get some plates and mugs and give everybody some crisps and Coke, and I'll tell youse all what happened."

Beady and Little Chan started cooking the sausages and beans and Suzie stopped glaring at the Nabber and began pouring out Coke in small quantities.

"Go on then," said the Nabber. "The suspense is killin'."

"The mugger was waitin' for me – last night – when I come back from Pa Richardson's. He got me and he knocked me down." Just talking about it brought it all back to Rocky, and he stopped talking.

"Sure he didn't crack yer on the head?"

"I'm warnin' yer, Nabber Neville!"

"Just another way of saggin' school."

"I don't think so," said Billy, accepting one crisp and an inch of Coke in a cup from Suzie. "Rocky's tellin' the truth. It's dangerous."

"Yer right, Billy," said Rocky. "And thanks fer believin' me – yer always was a good skin."

At that moment, the grill on the cooker erupted into flame and Little Chan hastily switched it off. A blue haze of smoke drifted lazily over their heads.

"These sausages is well done," said Beady. "Yer need a new cooker, Rocky."

"Oh, I don't know," said the Nabber, "it's pretty good at burnin' the cobwebs up there on the ceiling!"

"I warned yer!" said Rocky. "Told yer ter watch it!"

For a while, they watched the telly and ate the sausages and beans, but Rocky wasn't happy – he had a feeling the Cats were uneasy about something. At last Beady said, "Have ter tell yer something, Rocky."

The Nabber opened another can of Coke. "You tell him. Time he knew about it. He set it up."

"Chick and Spadge. Dey got me. They said ter tell yer the Sissler knew yer'd been in the deri and he wasn't happy."

"That's your fault," said the Nabber. "Writin' that stuff on the wall. Yer've got us in a right mess."

Rocky considered things. "Did they say anything about the loot?"

Beady shook his head.

"Den they don't know we took it. They would of said, if the Sissler had been in and found it gone. All the Sissler knows is I was in the deri and so was der loot. Doesn't mean *we* took it."

"He'll get around to that, Rocky," said Billy.

"No he won't. We'll get rid of the stuff anyway.

Yer seen that woman, Nabber?"

"These crisps is damp," said the Nabber, hedging. "Must be Pa Richardson's."

"Yer *haven't* seen her – and yer said yer could arrange it! Yer worth nothin', Nabber! Only thing yer good fer is blowin' up balloons – yer've got enough hot air!"

"I'll see her den," said the Nabber. "I'll see her!"

It wasn't easy phoning with his arm in a sling, but he got through.

"Mister – it's me – Rocky. It's that man … "

"Yes, Rocky?" The voice sounded very calm.

"He's been back – he got hold of me. I didn't tell him nothin'."

"Give me the number of the phone box you're in."

"What?"

"I'll phone you back."

"Right … "

After a few minutes the phone rang.

"Hello, mister."

"It was the same man?"

"Yes – I recognized him. Yer wouldn't recognize me, but – got me arm nearly broke and me face bashed in."

"I'm sorry about that, Rocky."

"Not as sorry as me. Listen, he wanted ter know where yer lived and listen, yer sure he's just a mugger? I mean, what's he want yer address for? So's he can mug yer again? He could mug anybody,

couldn't he? It's something else, in't it? He's a
terrorist, in't he? We've had terrorists round here –
at Mrs Aber's – and yer mixed up with them, in't
yer?"

"Hold on, Rocky, hold on."

"Nothin' ter hold on to – I'm sick of this – I'm
goin' ter the scuffers 'bout it."

There was a pause, then the man said, "I have to
ask you to do one dangerous thing."

"Yer mean it hasn't been dangerous up ter now?
It's been the big dipper! And I've had enough. Der's
just one thing yer can do – that twenty pound ... "

"Rocky." The man's voice was insistent. "Keep a
cool head and listen. It's very important you go
through with this. I'm relying on you. That man
will come back to you. When he does, don't resist."

"But, mister ... "

"It will be the last time. Give him this address.
Can you write it down?"

"Nothing to write with, but."

"Remember it. The Oaks. Sefton Drive."

"The what?"

"Oaks – oaks." The man sounded impatient.
"Trees."

"Them oaks. Never seen one."

"That doesn't matter. Now, if he comes again,
tell him that's my address. He'll want you to go
with him. Can you do that?"

"But, mister ... "

"I promise you – you'll be all right."

The phone went dead. Rocky slumped against the

wall of the telephone box. What was he caught up in, he wondered. Made yer sweat. It was what the wingy was singing about – missiles from heaven. He'd certainly got them.

CHAPTER

12

CONSTABLE McMahon and the wingy were outside Mrs Aber's, engaged in serious conversation. Rocky would have done a disappearing act, but they turned round and saw him. There was something about them, the way they looked at him and the way the wingy was shaking his head that worried Rocky, especially when he thought of the loot in the hideout, just a few yards away.

Deciding quickly on his tactics, he limped towards number 3, shouting across, in a suitably subdued way for walking wounded, "Hullo dur, Mr Oliver. How's things?" But Mr Oliver didn't reply and Constable McMahon started moving towards him. Rocky didn't pause and he'd almost got home when the policeman's voice said behind him, "Been in the wars, Rocky?"

Rocky turned to him with a frail smile. "Fell down the Steps the other night."

"Fell on yer face?"

"That's right. Hurt me arm as well. Been off school."

"Sorry about that, but I'll still have ter ask yer some questions, Rocky. Down at the station. Better have yer mother with us."

Straight away Rocky went on to the attack. "What's me mam got ter do with anything? What yer on about? What yer mean – questions? *I've* done nothin'." But he was thinking about the loot and the comic he'd pinched – and Lewis's. Which one had the scuffers got on to?

"Come on, Rocky."

Rocky pushed the policeman's hand from his shoulder. "That's me sore arm – geroff it, will yer? It's disgustin'! Youse lot owe me ... I got Jim Simpson for yer ... yer owe me ... "

Ellen-from-upstairs was putting Trevor in his pram. She clutched him to her and stared at Rocky and McMahon. "All right, Rocky?" she asked, nervously. "All right, is it?"

Rocky didn't reply. He stalked into the passage muttering, "Yer'll regret this, McMahon," and went into the living-room, startling his mother who was sitting by the fire drinking coffee and immersed in one of her romantic novels. She looked up at them, dazed.

"What's this?"

"Mrs Flanagan ... " began McMahon, but Mrs Flanagan leapt out of her chair. "What's he done now? What's he done? *I* can't keep control of him. He'll have ter go into a home. It's all Flanagan's fault. He shouldn't have gone off ... "

"Mrs Flanagan," said the constable, formally, "I have to ask you to come down to the station with Rocky. We're making some inquiries."

"Inquiries? What yer mean inquiries?"

"Just a matter of a few questions."

"I've done nothin', mam," protested Rocky. "Nothin'! They've just got it in for me! I'll take them out for it!"

Several neighbours had assembled outside to see what was happening. It enlivened a dull day to see Rocky and his mother taken off and also confirmed their opinion about that lot at number 3. Mrs Flanagan was in tears, like a mother at her daughter's wedding, sobbing, "He's got beyond me! I can't do nothin' with him!"

"Shurrup, mam," muttered Rocky.

Mr Oliver joined them as they passed Mrs Aber's. "Like to come along, Mac," he said. "The lad's got no father."

There was something about the way McMahon agreed to this that worried Rocky even more. It *had* to be the loot. Then he thought, there's no proof it's *my* hideout, anyway. Could be anybody's. To keep his spirits up, he kicked an empty can out of his way. "It's a waste," he said, "waste of the tax-payers' money, this is. Yer should be out after *real* criminals!"

"Know everything these days, don't yer?" said McMahon.

The sergeant at Larkspur Lane police station looked out over the desk calmly at a demented Mrs Flanagan and a very belligerent Rocky with a bruised mouth and his arm in a sling.

"What yer done to yerself, Rocky?" he asked.

"None of your business."

"What yer had us dragged down here for?" demanded Mrs Flanagan.

"Now then, Mrs Flanagan, just wanted to ask Rocky a few questions," he said, soothingly.

"Not answering any," retorted Rocky. "Youse can lock me up, but I'm not answering," and he leant against the wall, scowling but anxious.

"I can't do nothin' … " began Mrs Flanagan, but the sergeant interrupted. "If you'll just go into that room. Get a WPC, McMahon. And, Dave, yer'll have ter stay out here … "

In the detention room, Rocky and his mother sat down at the table and Constable McMahon sat opposite them. It was very bare and bleak and intimidating. Even McMahon seemed to find it intimidating. "Like a cuppa?" he asked.

Mrs Flanagan brightened up as a woman police constable brought in two mugs of tea, but Rocky pushed his away. "Youse is not bribin' me," he stated firmly, and glared at McMahon. "Come on den, scuffer," he said. "What's dis all about?"

Constable McMahon sighed. "Right, Rocky. Can yer tell me where yer were last Wednesday afternoon?"

Rocky scowled, thinking about it. Then it dawned on him. They hadn't done the deri on Wednesday – Wednesday was when …

"Was with me mam at the Pier Head. We was

seeing Flanagan off," he said.

Mrs Flanagan stopped crying. "That's right. He was. Yer can check that ... "

"We will." The constable seemed less confident. "Can yer give us the time?"

"We went down on the bus at two o'clock and we saw Flanagan's ship go about three ... "

"Then me mam went to me auntie Chrissie's ... "

"There's no need ter bring yer auntie Chrissie into this!"

"Well yer did, and me and Suzie got the bus home and it was about four o'clock and Beady's uncle was drivin' and ... " Suddenly it hit Rocky. "It's that old woman in the red woolly hat, in't it? She was on the Boulevard when they were bringing that old man out – it's her, in't it? She said I did him. She's a nutter! And yer believe her! And I saved her from the tiddlers in Joseph Terrace! And youse took me in when I've got a sore arm!" Relieved and indignant, he stood up. "I want a lawyer and compensation!"

"That's right. That's what we want!" agreed his mother, righteously. "And yer can keep yer tea!" And she pushed the half-empty mug away from her. "Arresting a sick lad! Yer always on to us, ever since Joey ... "

"Nothin' ter do with Joey, mam!"

The constable looked at them thoughtfully, then said, "One thing needs clearing up, Rocky. The old man's money was mainly in twenty pound notes. Now you've been trying to change one – that right?"

133

"A twenty pound note?" gasped Mrs Flanagan. "He's never even had a fiver ... Wur'd he get a twenty? Here!" She turned to Rocky, suddenly suspicious. "Mr Oliver said something about me havin' a ... "

"Will yer turn yer pockets out, Rocky?"

Rocky looked steadily at the constable, assessing the situation. Wasn't the old woman – was Pa Richardson and Mrs Chan as well – had to be. He couldn't see any way out of the situation. He made a last stand. "Youse can put me up against the wall and search me, den."

"Come on, Rocky. No need for that. What's in yer pockets?"

Rocky made his mind up. He pulled out the contents of his pockets and dropped them on the table: one used bus ticket; one membership card for the Baptist Youth Club; one biro – black; two pieces of chalk – white; one piece of string; one card with a number written on it, and one twenty pound note. Mrs Flanagan put her head down on the table and wept. "Oh, my God," she sobbed.

"Come on now, Rocky. Where did that twenty pound come from?" asked McMahon. "Didn't drop off the back of a lorry, did it?"

Rocky relaxed and sat back in the chair. Wasn't the gear in the hideout. Wasn't the comic he'd pinched. Wasn't Lewis's. Wasn't nothing he'd done wrong. It was saving that man's life.

"Wus give ter me," he said.

"Give ter yer? Yer mean somebody just handed

yer a twenty pound note?"

Rocky grinned. "That's right," he said. Was the truth after all.

"Now listen, son, we're trying to do the best for yer. But fairy tales went out a long time back. Did yer get it from Chick and Spadge?"

Rocky was interested. "Yer think Chick and Spadge did the old man? Well, they could of. But they told me dey was goin' straight."

"Was it Chick and Spadge?"

"No – it wasn't."

"Was it yer brother Joey?"

Mrs Flanagan brightened up. "It could of been Joey," she said. "Joey's been earnin' good money. In the Antarctic."

McMahon turned to her in disbelief. "The Antarctic? Joey?"

Mrs Flanagan got flustered. "Well no – I've got it wrong. It was Canada."

"Mrs Flanagan," said the constable, wearily, "we know Joey's been round Blackpool and Birkenhead and he's got a flash bike and a flash bike was seen outside Mr Selby's flat the night he was done."

Mrs Flanagan flared up. "Yer a lot of liars!" she shouted.

"Shurrup, mam!" said Rocky. "Wasn't Joey," he said to McMahon. "Wasn't Joey give me the twenty. Never give me nothing, Joey."

"Well, where did yer get it?"

"Tell yer tomorrow."

"Tomorrow's no good. We have ter know now."

"Typical! Yer've always got ter know everythin' straight off!"

"For yer own good, Rocky."

"For youse yer mean!" Rocky glared at him. The room was quiet and tense. Then McMahon said, "I'll get Mr Oliver."

When Mr Oliver came in he said nothing at first, then he said, "Rocky, will yer talk ter *me*?"

"Can't, Mr Oliver."

"Yer not holdin' anything against *me*, are yer? All I told Mac was that that twenty pound note was yer mother's that Flanagan give her. That's right, in't it? That's what yer told me."

Mrs Flanagan stood up. "Flanagan give me – he never give me ... What yer on about?" She turned on Rocky. "Wur'd yer get it? I'll batter yer! I'll belt yer round the Square for this!"

"Shurrup, mam," said Rocky, quietly, thinking what he should do. "Listen, scuffer," he said to the constable, "yer have ter let me phone somebody. Private, like. Then I'll tell youse."

Constable McMahon went out and Mrs Flanagan leaned across to Rocky. "Wur d'yer get it?" she whispered. "Wus it Flanagan? What yer been up to and not tellin' me – *me*, yer mother!"

Rocky only watched the glass panel in the door, waiting for McMahon to come back. It could all go wrong. The man with the white hair mightn't be there when he phoned – if they let him phone. Or he might say he didn't give him the twenty. He would have had it then!

136

The constable and the sergeant appeared at the glass panel, talking to each other, but looking in at Rocky speculatively. Rocky looked down at the table, then at his desert-wellies and hastily pushed his feet out of sight under the table. The desert-wellies could be a give-away.

"Yer know I've been pushed for money," his mother whispered, "and yer had all that and yer didn't even ... "

"Shurrup, mam!"

"I'll shurrup yer! Wait till I tell Flanagan!" Then she glared at the WPC sitting quietly in a corner. "And what *you* doin' here? Listenin' in ter people ... !"

"Mrs Flanagan ... " began Mr Oliver, but then McMahon came back.

"This way, Rocky," he said, in a reasonable sort of voice, indicating that Rocky could try it on once.

They let him use the phone at the sergeant's desk and they left him alone. He didn't need the card with the number on it – he knew it now. But it was a different voice that answered.

"Hi, mister – I want the man that – the man that ... " Rocky was sweating.

"Who is it?"

"Me – Rocky. Rocky O'Rourke."

"Wait."

Rocky waited – it seemed for ages. And he knew that the sergeant and McMahon were just on the other side of the door, ready to pounce. If the man didn't come across, he was landed.

"Rocky – what's happened?"

It was the man with white hair and Rocky started talking fast. "Listen, mister. It's not the mugger. It's the scuffers. Down Larkspur Lane. They've took me in because they think I pinched the twenty. Listen – yer'll have ter tell them … "

"You're speaking from the police station?"

"That's right … "

"You're certain of that?"

"What yer mean? Think I don't know it when I'm in it? They're goin' ter put me away!"

"You didn't give my number?"

Rocky scowled at the phone. "What yer mean? Promised I wouldn't, didn't I? Think I'm a grass?"

There was a long silence, then the man said, "No, Rocky. I don't think *you're* a grass. Ring off now and tell whoever's in charge I'll phone back in five minutes."

The line went dead. I'm in for it, Rocky thought. Then he went back to the detention room. "He's phoning yer back," he said to the sergeant.

When the sergeant returned to the detention room, Rocky, his mother and the wingy tried to read the sergeant's face, which was unreadable. He went to the table and gathered up the contents of Rocky's pockets and stood looking down in a funny sort of assessing way at Rocky. "Right, lad. Yer cleared. Yer can have all this back. We've nothing against yer."

Mrs Flanagan stood up, full of righteous rage.

138

"Nothin' against him! What yer mean nothin' against him after yer've dragged us through the streets in front of the neighbours? I'll have the law on youse!"

"Ah, come on, mam!" Rocky was sagging with relief. He just wanted out before the scuffers got on to something else. And the sergeant was still watching him speculatively. "Mind how yer go, Rocky," he said, enigmatically.

Rocky turned on him, squaring up. "What yer mean mind how I go? What yer mean? Yer said yer've got nothin' on me! So come on – or belt up! Come on – I've only got one good arm, but I'll take yer on with that!" and Rocky danced round, punching out with one threatening fist.

"Yer've got me scared, Rocky," said the sergeant, "but remember what I said. Mind how yer go."

The wingy stayed behind when Rocky and his mother left. "What's it all about?" he asked the sergeant.

"I feel sorry for that lad. He's got guts, but what'll become of him? Pity his step-father had to go away." He rested his elbow on his desk and rubbed his nose reflectively. "Better keep an eye on him, Dave – and you, McMahon."

"But what's it all about?" repeated the wingy.

"Can't tell yer, Dave. It's confidential. But the twenty pound is legitimate. He's done nothin' wrong. At least," he added, "not so far as the money's concerned."

"What's goin' on? What's all this phonin'? And the

twenty pounds?" demanded Mrs Flanagan as she went home with Rocky. "I've got a right to know. Yer've got in with somebody like Jim Simpson, haven't yer? Some gang. I don't know what Flanagan'll say ... "

"Wouldn't say nothin', would he? Can't even write to us."

"He's a long way away but. And *I* know," Mrs Flanagan sobbed, "*I* know if he *could*, he *would*!"

"Look!" Rocky pushed his hand through his hair desperately, "the scuffers clarified me – didn't they? Yer heard them, didn't yer?"

"Yes, but ... "

"I'm goin' off this!" Rocky started away ahead of her, but she caught up with him, saying confidentially, "Rocky, I don't care where yer got the twenty from really, but can yer lend me a few pounds? Just till the end of the week, like? I'm a bit short."

Rocky thought about it. He could do a deal. He could give his mother the twenty and let her buy something with it so she got it changed and the rest would be his. But it wasn't worth the risk. She might lose the lot on bingo or give it to Joey. Better to keep it. Anyway, he was worried about what the sergeant had said – "Mind how yer go." Must be the terrorist. He couldn't do anything about the terrorist. But he could get rid of that loot. And he'd have to find another place to hide the twenty now his mother knew about it.

CHAPTER
13

"He's been done," said Beady, confirming the rumour that had gone round the school that day. "It's definite. Me mam saw the scuffers takin' him away – him *and* his mam."

"What they want his mam for?" asked the Nabber. "What *she* done?"

"It's the law," said Billy, earnestly. "If yer a juvenile, yer have ter have a parent with yer." For the first time, the Nabber was impressed by Billy and Billy felt this. "It'll be the gear from the Rialto. I warned Rocky about it. It's handlin' stolen goods."

"We all handled them, but," said Beady and Billy nodded and gripped the handlebars of his bike so hard his knuckles were white.

Little Chan was numb just thinking what his parents would say if *he* was arrested as well. Even the Nabber was anxious, though he didn't show it. He just went on chewing and looking into the window of the newsagent's on Larkspur Lane. "We'll be all right. He'll not scat on us. We just keep clear of the hideout," he said. "And if the scuffers come askin' questions, we deny everything. And the night we did the Rialto we was all together – us lot – "

"Where were we?" asked Beady. "We've got ter have the same story."

"We was – we was *here*," said the Nabber, desperately. "We was standin' here talkin' and that."

"An' I suppose *she* was watching us," said Beady, indicating the woman with the scarf round her head and the cigarette in her mouth who was looking out at them from behind the counter.

"Well – Pa Richardson's then!"

The Cats said nothing. They knew they hadn't got an alibi. Little Chan, who was just back from the Chinese centre, played a few mournful notes on his flute, which did nothing for the Cats' spirits.

"Hi – listen youse!" They turned at the sound of Rocky's voice, and crowded round asking questions. What was he taken in for? – was it the loot? – what was he let out for? – who'd clatted?

"Cool it!" said Rocky. "Wasn't the loot and they've got nothin' on me and it was Pa Richardson and your mam, Chan, that clatted about that twenty pound note."

Little Chan's face crumpled in dismay. "My mam wouldn't clat – she's not a clatter!" he protested.

"Who else would know about the twenty, but?" demanded Rocky.

The Nabber, who had stopped chewing in relief that it wasn't the gear in the hideout, started chewing again. "Might have known it! The mugger again!"

Rocky ignored this, having other business on his mind. "Listen, youse, the gear's got ter go," he said. "Yer can't tell where the scuffers'll stop. What's that woman say that yer said would take it, Nabber?"

"What yer on about now?"

"The woman yer said ... " Rocky turned away in disgust. "There's no woman, is there? Never was. Like the man that would sell yer ... "

"Oh, *her*?" The Nabber pretended to get his memory back. "She's gone. Not my fault. Not my fault if she's gone, is it?"

Rocky didn't say anything, but he started thinking while the others protested.

"My mam's not a clatter," Little Chan repeated quietly.

"It's stolen stuff, Rocky," said Billy.

"Was your idea, takin' it," the Nabber reminded him.

"Come on, we was all in it," said Beady.

Rocky came to a decision. "Right. It'll have ter go back."

"Ter the Rialto?" asked the Nabber, derisively.

"When?" asked Beady.

"Now. Just start gettin' it ready! Unless the great Nabber Neville has some other idea for gettin' rid of it."

The Nabber shrugged – he hadn't.

When Ellen-from-upstairs opened the door, the young fellow was behind her. "Hello dur, Rocky. Scuffers let yer go, luv? All right, is it?" she asked. "I've just been with yer mam. She's in hysterics."

"Can I borrow the pram again, Ellen – just fer an hour?"

143

"Well, I don't know, Rocky. What wur yer taken in for?" And the young fellow asked, "What yer want it for?"

"What's it ter do with *you*?" Rocky demanded. "Not your pram. Listen, Ellen, I've done nothin' wrong, see. Was a mistake the scuffers takin' me in."

"I don't want ter get mixed up in anything."

"Yer'll not be. It's just for the guy. Just for an hour. Honest. Won't harm the pram. Ah, come on, Ellen!"

Ellen still hesitated, but she could feel Rocky's anxiety.

"All right, well. Yer can have it. I'll bring Trevor in. Did yer make much last time?"

"Wasn't bad."

"Well, yer could buy Trevor a little present if yer do all right again."

What would I buy Trevor a present for, wondered Rocky as he rattled the old pram down to the hideout. Not Trevor's pram, was it? Buy something for Ellen – was *her* pram after all, and she was a good skin.

The same procession went along Princes Boulevard – Little Chan in the Nabber's hat sitting in the pram on top of the loot; Beady pushing the pram because of Rocky's arm; the Nabber and Rocky alongside and Billy cycling behind. They didn't stop to ask for pennies for the guy.

"Load of nothin' this is," grumbled the Nabber.

"We take it out and we put it back. Brilliant! And I get paid double for night work."

"Your fault, Nabber," panted Rocky. "Wus *you* messed it up."

They got through Joseph Terrace without seeing Chick's Lot and the alley behind the Rialto was empty.

"Der's nobody in there," whispered Rocky, after listening for a moment outside the broken window. "I'll go in first, but yer'll have ter bunk me up, Beady, 'cos of me arm. Nabber, you come in next. Beady hand der stuff in and Billy keep dowse."

They were all sagging with relief when they got back from the Rialto into the courtyard of St Catherine's Buildings.

"That's it then," said Rocky. "We're clean!" And he danced in and out of the shadows in his desert-wellies. Except for the terrorist, his troubles were over. The police had cleared him, the gear was out of the hideout and he could change the twenty. "We're clean!" he shouted.

"An' what about the Sissler?" asked Beady.

"We've *done* the Sissler! Been in and out of his deri and he doesn't know it! Come on!"

And he started racing round the courtyard and the others followed him, shouting, and Billy cycled round and round ringing his bell. Then a window in the Buildings was opened and a man shouted, "Will youse lot shurrup and clear out!"

"Shurrup yerself!" shouted Rocky, indignantly.

"Shurrup! Shurrup!" shouted the Nabber and Beady.

"Have the police on ter yer!" And the window was closed, but then a door to one of the ground floor flats opened, spilling light out, and outlining the figure of a very large man. He stood quite still and said, menacingly, "Clear off."

"Who's he?" whispered Rocky.

"New caretaker," whispered Billy. "They say he used ter be a wrestler."

Rocky considered the matter. When the wingy had been caretaker there, he'd played footy with them in the courtyard, though no ball games were allowed. That had got him sacked – or helped to. This man was – well, yer couldn't take risks with him, that was clear. The Cats moved on through the courtyard.

"Have ter get home, Rocky," said Billy.

"What for, skin? Come on – we'll do somethin' … "

"I also must get home." Little Chan got out of the pram and gave the Nabber his hat back. "This pram isn't going properly."

"What's wrong with it?" asked Rocky anxiously.

"One wheel is wobbly."

"Was always wobbly."

"More wobbly than it was."

"Can't give it back to Ellen wobbly."

"Got me tool kit," said Billy. "I can fix it. Just needs a spanner."

They stood around while Billy fixed the wheel.

"That's great!" said Rocky when Billy was finished, pushing the pram up and down. "Great! Yer've done it, Billy."

"Was nothin'." Billy put his tool kit back on his bike. He knew Rocky would want to do something else now, but he was tired and his leg was aching. "Have ter go now," he said. "Terrah." And he went off on his bike.

"Terrah," said Little Chan.

Rocky, Beady and the Nabber watched them go, and the darkness and boredom of the evening pressed down on them. "Come on," said Rocky and started pushing the pram out of the gloom of the courtyard of St Catherine's, through the archway into the Square. Rocky was thinking fiercely about things. The last thing he wanted to do then was to go home. He put the pram into the passage of number 3 and came out. "Listen," he said. "We're doing a Free Food Here – down Larkspur Lane. Stir Pa Richardson up. He clatted on me."

"What yer on to now?" asked the Nabber.

"Yer'll see. We want some big bits of cardboard – can yer get them, Nabber?"

"Well, me dad's got some cardboard boxes in the shed."

"Get them. And, Beady, yer good at putting letters on things."

"Got a lot of fibre tips."

"Get them – and I'll get the scissors and string."

Under a lamp-post in the Square, the Nabber tore up cardboard boxes and Beady wrote "Free Food

Here" in big letters on each piece of cardboard and Rocky pierced holes in them with the scissors and threaded string through the holes. Then they went and tied a piece of cardboard on every lamp-post from the bottom of Joseph Terrace, past St Catherine's Buildings and down Larkspur Lane and left one propped up outside Pa Richardson's with an arrow pointing to his door. Then they retreated into the shadows and waited.

Three skin-heads came along first, following the notices. They looked in at Pa Richardson, then went inside, and Pa Richardson started arguing with them, and more people started coming and going into the shop and queuing outside and the skin-heads came out and threw something at the window, but it bounced off the wires.

Rocky and Beady and the Nabber fell about laughing, but then Rocky saw the old woman in the red woolly hat joining the noisy, pushing crowd at the shop and he ran over to her. She'd saved him from the terrorist and he didn't want her hurt.

"Hi, missus – don't go in. Der's no free food – just a joke, see?"

"What yer mean? Oh, I know *you*. You're the one that ... "

"Don't go in!"

"Yer little devil ... ! Clear off!"

"All right then! But I did my best for yer!"

Angrily Rocky stalked off, shoulders hunched, waving to the Nabber and Beady to follow him, and leaving the crowd still outside Pa Richardson's. He hadn't wanted to harm the old woman.

"That's it then," said the Nabber. "What we do now?"

"Come on," said Rocky, soberly. "We'll have a brew-up in the hideout. Come on," and he went with the Nabber and Beady up the Steps, shouting and laughing, but he was sorry about the old woman. She *had* clatted on him to the scuffers, but she'd also saved him from the terrorist, and he hadn't wanted to harm her.

"What's up wid *you* then?" asked the Nabber, sensing that Rocky wasn't happy.

"Nothin'," Rocky replied, and went first, cautiously as usual, down the steps into the hideout. He fumbled for the catch on the door – but the door was partly open and there was a strong smell of paraffin from inside. Silent as a shadow, Rocky went back up the stairs.

"Somebody's been in," he whispered. "Could still be in."

"We'll get them," hissed the Nabber.

"No. Youse wait here – and keep dowse," and Rocky ran off home to get his torch. They couldn't risk lighting a candle in the hideout if there was paraffin spilt ...

Rocky shone the torch round the hideout. The sofa had been ripped up, the card table broken and the playing cards scattered on the floor, soaking up the paraffin that had dripped down from the overturned stove. The postcards had been torn off the wall.

"It's a tip," said the Nabber. "Somebody must of clatted."

"None of us would of clatted," said Rocky.

"Must be Chick's Lot. Has ter be. They've been watching us."

"Never seen them round here but," said Beady.

They talked, but Rocky didn't. All he could think of was that *his* hideout, the place he was always safe in, that nobody but the Cats knew about, had been done. All the things he'd got together for it ripped up – even his father's postcards. He shone his torch round and Beady and the Nabber stopped talking as it lit up some writing on the wall done with black paint from an aerosol – "Bobby Sissley was here. Sissley is the Sissler. Bobby Sissley rules."

"Told yer," said the Nabber. "Didn't I tell yer? Dead give away what yer wrote in the Rialto."

"Must be that girl," said Beady. "Must be." But he wasn't sure.

"I'll find out," said Rocky. "*Termorrer* I'll find out."

CHAPTER
14

IN daylight – if you could call it daylight – Joseph Terrace looked a lot less dangerous. The off-licence and the pub were closed so the only lights were in the launderette at the corner where three women and two babies sat looking out of the window like fish in an aquarium. Newspapers like pale, overgrown cabbages sprouted in corners; grass and weeds, forcing their way through the concrete, were preparing to take the place over along with the broken bottles. On the wall of an empty house was written in big black lettering: "King Billy is a hero – the Boyne 1690" with a drawing of a man on a horse underneath. The sky was low and pallid and in the still air the washing hung out on the balconies of the Buildings was damp and drooping. One or two women looked down into the street while they gossiped and some tiddlers had got two supermarket trolleys and were riding them up and down the Terrace, with a good shove-off from friends.

Rocky pushed his hands into the pockets of his anorak and started down. It was foreign territory – and he knew it.

He made for one of the staircases in the Building

and the tiddlers saw him and abandoned their
trolleys in favour of him and surged round him.
"What yer want? Yer don't belong here," one of
them said.

"Clear off youse!" said Rocky fiercely.

The tiddlers didn't move, but another said, "Give
us a ciggy or we'll do yer!"

"Right," said Rocky, "try it on." He glared at
them with tiger-fierce eyes and they moved back a
bit. Then one of them said, "He's Rocky O'Rourke
– St Catherine's Square," and they pressed round
him again, but with more respect.

"Hi, Rocky, give us a ciggy. Give us a ciggy,
Rocky," they chanted.

Rocky looked round at them, his tiger-yellow
eyes narrowed. "Shurrup – all on youse," he ordered
and when they'd shut up he said, "Tell yer what I'll
do. Give ten pence ter the one of youse that tells me
where Bobby Sissley lives."

They didn't say anything, looking at him in a
quiet, wary way, then one of them asked, "Chick
an' Spadge know yer here?"

"What's Chick an' Spadge got ter do with it?"
demanded Rocky.

The tiddlers watched him without answering.
"Right," said Rocky, "youse all working for Chick
an' Spadge, that it?" And thinking about the loot in
the Rialto, he added, "Trannies and that?"

Still nobody said anything. Then one of the
tiddlers said in a quiet voice. "Der's a girl – Bobbie
Sissley – up there," and he pointed towards the top

floor flats. "Wur's the ten pence, but?"

"Hi, Rocky," said another one, pushing forward, "can I join the Cats gang?"

"Can *I* join?"

"Can *I*?"

"Don't take tiddlers in the Cats gang," said Rocky. "And clear off or I'll do *youse*!"

They dropped back.

"We was only messin', Rocky."

"Hi, Rocky, give us a ciggy!"

By the time Rocky got to the first-floor landing, they'd gone back to the trolleys, and Rocky went on up the stairs, thinking that Suzie was just a tiddler and maybe he should be taking more care of her or she might finish up like one of them. But he was pretty sure of one thing – those tiddlers were working for Chick and Spadge. They could easily have been trained to get things – like trannies out of cars, and a tiddler could lift anything from a shop without being noticed. But how did the Sissler fit into it?

A woman coming out of one of the flats asked him, suspiciously, "What yer doing here?"

"Lookin' for the Sissleys."

"Them!" She turned away contemptuously.

He went up to the next floor. It was quiet except for the shouts of the tiddlers below and music from one or two transistors. And he knew it was dangerous. Somewhere near here there was the Sissler and the tiddlers could have warned Chick and Spadge he was on their territory. He wouldn't put anything past those tiddlers.

He risked knocking on a door and a man opened it and looked at him. "What's this then?"

"Lookin' for a friend. Bobbie Sissley."

Again there was that look of contempt. "Her? Number 43. Next floor up."

Number 43 seemed empty. There was no sound of anybody and no noise. Rocky pressed the bell. Nothing happened. Then he saw the curtain at one window dropping back into place. He was being watched, but nobody came out. He wondered what he was into, but he wasn't going to give up and he pressed the bell again. He heard voices behind the door, then a key being turned and he braced himself for trouble. The door was opened on a chain, and Bobbie Sissley looked out at him, anxiously. Then she smiled, her face lighting up. "Rocky!" she said, and unfastened the chain and opened the door wide. "Hello dur, Rocky! Wur yer wantin' me? Are we playin' again?" And she turned and shouted, "It's Rocky, mam. Can he come in?" And then she turned back to him, "Me mam says yer can come in."

Rocky went in, reluctantly. It was a waste of time. He knew she wasn't the Sissler. You just had to hear her voice and see her face. He'd have to start again.

Bobbie Sissley locked and chained the door behind him, which gave Rocky a funny feeling. The flat was still and quiet except for the sound of a television in one of the rooms. And there was a feeling of fear.

"Like gettin' inter Walton Jail, this is," he said. "What's yer locked in for?"

And Bobbie's smile vanished. "Have ter be careful. They don't like us round here, see?" she said anxiously.

"What for?"

"Don't know. We haven't done nothing but they shout at us and we never go out at night and nobody has ter come in – except Chick and Spadge sometimes."

Rocky couldn't believe it. "Chick an' Spadge? Yer let them two in?"

"They've been very good, but. Ter me brother. They bring him things and talk to him."

"Chick an' Spadge? Bein' good?" He pushed his hand through his red hair so that it stood up on end. "Yer jokin'!"

"I'm not – they've been ... "

"They're not doin' that for nothin'. Yer brother go out with them?"

"He can't, see. Bobby's ... "

"Bobby?"

"Me brother. He's Bobby as well. We're twins, see?"

Rocky looked round the narrow hall and at the locked door. He felt trapped. He knew he'd found the Sissler. He was in the flat somewhere and he was in with Chick and Spadge, planning things, and using the tiddlers as well. He had to be clever, a big criminal, and working it all from this flat. Rocky's first impulse was to get out, but then he made up his mind – he would face the Sissler – he'd come to get him and he *would*.

"Let's see yer brother," he said.

"Come on then – this is his room. He'll be pleased ter see yer."

Whatever he'd expected, it wasn't what faced him. Bobbie took him into a small bedroom. There was a transistor playing quietly and a boy lying in a bed reading a book, and he was the image of Bobbie, except that he was a lot thinner and paler.

"Hi, Bobby," said Bobbie. "Here's Rocky ter see yer … "

The boy dropped his book and huddled under the bedclothes. He seemed to get even paler and his eyes darkened with fear.

CHAPTER

15

"THEY'RE twins," said Rocky.

"So they're *both* in on it? That's clever!" The Nabber, in the roller skates his father had just bought him, twirled round in a circle, skated along Larkspur Lane, came back and pulled up sharp.

Rocky watched him contemptuously. "Finished showin' off?" he asked. "This is serious. They're not in it together. Know nothin' about it. He's sick. In bed all the time."

"What's wrong with him, Rocky?" asked Billy.

"Don't know. But he doesn't look as if he'll get better."

"So who was writin' all this up about the Sissler?" asked Beady. "And who did the hideout?"

"Chick and Spadge. They've got the Sissleys terrified. They've been tellin' them everybody in Joseph Terrace hated them. Only ones to help them was Chick and Spadge."

"Sissleys believed that? That's crazy!"

"They've not been there long. They just believed Chick and Spadge and Chick and Spadge set people against them – especially the tiddlers, see? So I told them about Chick and Spadge and then the Sissleys wanted ter go straight ter the scuffers."

"Great!" said the Nabber. "That's great! Now yer've really got us in trouble! The Sissleys go ter the scuffers, the scuffers come to us and we have ter tell them about the Rialto and gettin' the loot and ... I'm emigratin'."

Rocky leant back against the wire frames on Pa Richardson's window. "I'm tellin' yer, Nabber. The Sissleys is leavin' it ter me. What we'll do is, we'll tell Chick and Spadge ter lay off the Sissleys and lay off us, see? We'll have ter have a meetin' with them. Can yer arrange it, Billy?"

"Yer mean a fight?" Billy was anxious. He hated it when they had a fight.

"Don't need ter fight them."

"I get it," said the Nabber, trying not to show that he was worried as well about meeting Chick's Lot, "we just ask them to stop it – politely. So I'll bring me dad's big hammer, just in case."

Rocky scowled at him. "Bring what yer like. But yer won't need it. I've got it all worked out. Can yer arrange a meeting with dem, Billy?"

"I'll try."

"Do it meself if yer worried."

"Not worried." And Billy sat up straight on his bike.

"Right then. And watch out for them tiddlers in Joseph's – they're crazy. Day after tomorrow for the meeting, Billy. See youse." But then, as the Cats split up to go home, Rocky stopped Little Chan. "Hi," he said, confidentially, "yer dad know Kung Fu?"

Little Chan looked into Rocky's face searchingly and reluctantly shook his head.

"He has to – he's Chinese," said Rocky, beginning to feel worried.

"He has a book about it," said Little Chan, helpfully. "A very old one – with pictures."

"A book?" Rocky was doubtful. "Well – it might be all right."

"But it is in Chinese."

"That's great. Real great!"

Rocky went home feeling desperate. He could see his whole plan disintegrating – it would be a disaster. Then, in the Square, he saw Mr Oliver on his way for a pint and he shouted after him, hopefully, "Hi, Mr Oliver."

"Hello, dur, Rocky. How's the arm?"

"S'all right now. Mr Oliver, did you used to do wrestlin'? I mean – I mean before yer accident? Could yer teach me?"

"Could teach yer boxing, Rocky. Are yer interested?"

"Boxin's no good," said Rocky, despondently.

The wingy was indignant. "Boxin' no good? What yer mean? It's the finest ... "

"Nothin' against boxin', Mr Oliver. But I – well, self-defence sort of thing – it was that ... "

Mr Oliver thought about it. "Not a bad idea ter be able ter defend yerself, Rocky, but I can't help yer there. Yer could try a class."

"A class?" Rocky scowled. He could just see himself in some judo class doing what he was told –

what everybody else was being told. "Not my scene, Mr Oliver. Anyway, it'd take too long," he concluded. "Thanks, but," and he turned away.

"Here – Rocky," Mr Oliver shouted after him. "Got another idea. There's Constable McMahon – he's got a belt for judo."

"Der scuffer?" Rocky was scornful. "He'll lock me up before he'll help me."

"Think yer wrong, Rocky. He's not bad, McMahon. And he knows yer."

"Knows I've cheeked him."

"He's not one ter hold that against yer. Not if yer really serious. I could have a word with him."

Mr Oliver watched anxiously while Rocky considered things, and Rocky was thinking that McMahon was his last hope if he was going to fix Chick's Lot.

"Right," he said. "I'll try him. See him about it meself, but. All right?" Never trust a scuffer, he reminded himself as he went down to the police station.

Constable McMahon was just going off duty when he was confronted by a desperate-looking Rocky in the bleak, neon-lit passageway of the police station.

"In trouble again, lad?" he asked. "What's it? Suzie run off?"

"Not that." Rocky glared at him ferociously. "Der wingy told me yer've got a belt for judo. That right?"

"Got two."

"Congratulations. Can yer learn me one or two things?"

McMahon became curious, as Rocky knew he would.

"What for?" he asked. "Got a problem?"

"Want ter know how ter defend meself – if I have to. What's wrong with that? Anyway," Rocky went on, getting angry, "I can go elsewhere, but youse owe me – I got Jim Simpson for youse and youse just arrested me when I'd done nothin' and … "

"All right, all right," McMahon knew from what the Sergeant had said that Rocky could be in some danger and he had a sneaking admiration for Rocky – Rocky always bounced back, whatever happened. "I'll make a concession for yer. I'll teach yer one or two things – but just to defend yerself, nothin' else. Right? Take yer down ter the police gym tomorrow."

Rocky was suspicious. "The police gym?"

"Look, Rocky, I can't teach yer here – or out in the street."

"Suppose not. But listen, if I have somebody bigger than me comin' at me – can yer show me how to get him down on his back?"

"Show yer tomorrow."

"That's great!" Rocky shouted, in relief. "That's great! Never thought I'd get help from a scuffer!"

"Listen, lad, don't get too happy. Yer not goin' to enjoy it, I'm warnin' yer. It'll be hard work. I'll put yer down twenty times, but then yer'll be able ter put *me* down. Promise yer."

Rocky was fascinated – him put a scuffer down! "Hi!" he shouted. "Hi, if I can put *you* down, I can put any scuffer down! See yer, den!"

Jubilant – and hungry – he went home without a thought of the terrorist as he ran up the Steps, his imagination divided between what his mother might have dreamt up for tea and how he was going to get his own back – permanently – on Chick and Spadge. Thanks to McMahon he could see himself throwing Spadge over his shoulder, could hear Spadge crying and groaning, could see himself doing the same for Chick and then – but no, that wasn't how to do it. He'd have to get his plans clear. The plan would be his, but he had to thank McMahon for making it possible. Like streaky bacon were scuffers – and a streaky bacon butty wouldn't be a bad idea for the tea.

Suzie was digging a hole with an old spoon in the abandoned garden in the Square. Beside her, on the ground, lay something covered with a duster. Rocky stopped. "What yer doin', tatty-'ead?" he asked.

She smiled up at him. "Dead, Rocky," she said. "Dead!" And she picked up the duster and there was the Barbie doll. Rocky dropped on to the ground beside her. "Yer not ... yer crazy, Suzie! Yer not buryin' it?"

Suzie nodded, happily. "Dead," she repeated and carefully laid the doll in the hole she had dug and started spooning soil over it. Then she went to pick some weeds and stuck them into the ground over Barbie. "Gone," she said. "All gone."

"Yer give me the creeps – honest! I'm not buying yer any dolls – not if yer goin' ter bury them."

"Buy somethin' else," Suzie suggested anxiously.

"Oh – come on!"

But his mother was out again, the doors were locked and Ellen-from-upstairs was out and had taken Trevor with her. Rocky pushed his hand desperately through his hair and went to sit down on the doorstep. What's up with her, he wondered. She's never in these days – not when she's wanted. What's she up to? Could have her up for neglect, especially if the pies and beans were taken into consideration.

Suzie sat down beside him. "Went out," she said, helpfully.

"Where to?"

"Out," Suzie explained.

"I *know* she's out, tatty-'ead! Wur to, but? And when'll she come back?"

"Not come back," said Suzie, hopefully.

Well, Rocky decided, I'm not sitting here looking at Barbie's grave and the old car and the builder's hut all night. He cast his mind about for places to go to. The wingy would let him stay at his place, but his wife wouldn't. Ellen was out and he wasn't popular with any of the Cats' parents at the moment. Hideout was no good either.

"Hungry," said Suzie.

"Not the only one."

Then he thought of the Baptist Youth Club. He could get tea and biscuits. Have to take Suzie though, and she'd got a fair amount of soil over herself burying Barbie. Still, it was worth a try and he could check up on the Christmas party.

He stood up – "Come on, tatty-'ead!" he shouted, and started running.

The door of the Baptist Hall was open. Some boys were putting up the table-tennis table and the tea cups and milk and sugar were set out on a table near the kitchen. Just in case things didn't work out, Rocky put a handful of biscuits in his pocket and was stopping Suzie from doing the same when Betty Mulloney came out of the kitchen and, seeing him, cast a suspicious eye over the table.

Rocky hated having to suck up to Betty Mulloney, but it had to be done. "Can we have some tea, Betty?" he asked persuasively.

"*She* can't," said Betty. "She's not a member and she's dirty. Anyway, the tea's not served for half an hour. That's when we have it."

Rocky tried not to get angry. "S'all right – we'll wait."

"*She* can't wait – she's not ... "

"She's waitin' with me," said Rocky, fiercely, and Betty Mulloney looked disdainful and prepared to stand guard over the table.

"Here," Rocky demanded, "when's the Christmas party?"

"We're not havin' one. If yer'd come to the last meetin' yer would know that. We're invitin'

164

Senior Citizens instead."

Rocky was bewildered. "Senior Citizens? What yer mean? What yer want Senior Citizens for?"

"Mr Ferndean suggested that *we* could do without a Christmas Party and bring a lot of happiness to the old folk by giving them a treat," said Betty, virtuously. "And we agreed."

"But what about me subs?" demanded Rocky, indignantly. "It's not *his* money he's playin' about with!"

"D'yer not understand? We're all givin' up the subs for the sake of the Senior Citizens. *If* yer've paid yer subs yer can invite a Senior ... "

Rocky sidestepped the question of his subs.

"Right! I'm bringin' one. I'm havin' me money's worth!"

"Yer too late," replied Betty, with calm satisfaction. "All the tickets were allotted at the last meeting."

"Wur's Mr Ferndean? I'm havin' this out with him!"

"In his office ... "

He wasn't, but there was a neat pile of pink tickets on his desk. He picked one up and read it. "The Youth Club invites you to a Senior Citizens' Christmas Tea on 20th December at 3.30 p.m. in the Baptist Hall. Please bring this ticket and a friend with you." Rocky thought about it. He couldn't stop it, but he could have a ticket and he helped himself to one from the bottom of the pile. They'd never miss it and he'd got nothing to lose anyway – he wouldn't be coming back to the Youth Club –

wasn't worth it now.

Suzie followed him along Princes Boulevard, shouting, "Party!" and waving a pink ticket.

"Der's no ... Here, wur'd yer ... Give us that! Yer shouldn't of took it, Suzie!"

"You take!"

"That's different – I'd paid me subs – oh, never mind!"

Suzie began to cry. "Party," she wailed.

"Listen, tatty-'ead, der's no party, but I'm buying yer a present but yer'll not get it if yer don't shurrup! And here's a biscuit."

On the way home, he called in at the house where the old woman in the red woolly cap lived. There was a woman brushing the front path who looked at them suspiciously.

"What yer want?"

"The old woman in the red woolly cap – where's she live? Which is her place?"

"What yer want her for?"

"That's *my* business, missus."

"Well, yer can clear off – we've had enough trouble with your kind."

Rocky scowled. "I just want ter give her this invitation. Here ... " He got out his biro and wrote on the back of the card, "This is from the one that baters his sister and take Mr Selby as well."

"Give her this," he said, "and tell her it's for saving my life."

"Who d'yer think yer coddin', yer little ... "

"Not coddin'. You tell her!"

And Suzie shouted one of her more objectionable remarks as they ran off.

Who could they give the other ticket to, he wondered as they ran home. Maybe his mam? But she wasn't a Senior Citizen yet, he didn't think. But there was the wingy. He could be a Senior Citizen. Then he slowed down, thinking about the meeting with Chick's Lot, going over the plans he had for it. Have to practise what McMahon taught him. Have to. If things didn't work out, they'd all be slaughtered, the Cats.

CHAPTER

16

THE waste ground behind the old houses in Joseph Terrace was dark. The only light was from a street lamp on the Terrace. The Cats waited by the back of one of the houses. There was no sign of Chick's Lot.

"Know what yer up to?" asked the Nabber.

"Shut up," hissed Rocky.

"Shut up!" echoed Suzie, jumping up and down beside Rocky with a half brick in her hand.

"Doin' all this for the Sissler," muttered the Nabber.

"Doin' it for *us* – for the hideout," retorted Rocky.

"Hideout has been done," whispered Little Chan.

"Won't be done again," said Rocky.

Just beside the pavement in Joseph Terrace, Billy was keeping dowse. He was hoping Chick's Lot wouldn't show up.

The Cats kept very still, clutching their sticks. Rocky had said they should do nothing until he told them. It wasn't easy, waiting. Then Billy saw something – just a shadow – moving at the other end of the waste ground. He couldn't see anything very clearly, but it looked like a lot of people. The

Cats wouldn't have a chance against all that lot. And Rocky had to be warned. Billy hooted – very quietly.

"That's it," said Rocky. "Come on."

"Come on!" shouted Suzie.

"Shurrup, will yer, Suzie!"

The Cats moved slowly across the waste ground towards the group of figures coming towards them.

"There's hundreds of them," muttered the Nabber. "We'll be shredded!"

"They must have the tiddlers with them," said Beady.

"Stop here," said Rocky, and the Cats waited as Chick's Lot came towards them.

Chick's voice came out of the darkness. "Right then, kittens. What yer want? What yer on our territory for?"

"*Your* territory? Thought it was the Sissler's territory. Got the Sissler with yer? Want to talk to him."

There was a moment's silence, then Chick shouted, "Think the Sissler'd bother with youse lot?"

"No!" shouted Rocky. "Knew he would send *you*. Yer workin' for him, aren't yer? Yer the Sissler's Lot now, aren't youse? Youse and the tiddlers! Took youse all over, hasn't he? Sissler rules, doesn't he?"

There was another pause while Chick thought things over again, then he shouted, "We'll show yer who rules!" and there was a loud yelling.

"Better get out," muttered the Nabber. "No way

we can beat them!"

"S'all right," Rocky whispered, tensely. "I've got a plan."

"Yer always have – and it always goes wrong!" protested Nabber.

"Show yer, Nabber. Stop here." The Cats waited as Chick's Lot and the tiddlers came towards them.

Rocky was as worried as the rest of the Cats, but he flexed his muscles and started up again. "Settlin' this, Chick! Me and Spadge! Tergether. He wins, it's yours."

They could hear Chick and Spadge laughing, then Spadge shouted, "I'm terrified! Terrified – aren't I, Chick?"

"I'm not. Come on!" retorted Rocky.

"Don't do it, Rocky," whispered Beady. "He's bigger than you."

"The size," said Rocky, "is not important. Keep hold of Suzie," and he started off towards the neutral ground between the two gangs. But his mouth was dry with fear – Spadge *was* a lot bigger than he was. All he could do was to keep repeating to himself what McMahon had told him – grip tight, fall back and hold, turn over and twist and hold ...

Spadge was coming towards him, a dark figure whirling a bicycle chain over his head, and Chick's Lot and the tiddlers were shouting encouragement. Grip tight, fall back and hold, turn over and hold, Rocky told himself, and then stood his ground and let Spadge come on until he was standing over him and Rocky could hear the cycle chain whipping the air above him. Then he suddenly reached up and grabbed Spadge's arm and fell back on to the ground pulling Spadge down with him and threw his right leg over Spadge and heaved over and sat astride Spadge, pinning both his arms down. Spadge gave a surprised grunt and then said, "Geroff, yer little ... " and started struggling. Rocky held him down desperately, but Spadge got an arm free and pushed his hand into Rocky's face, forcing him backwards, and Rocky, his lungs panting for breath, thought he'd had it, but he remembered McMahon's voice – "Don't panic – both hands on one arm, fall back, twist and turn ... turn him and turn yerself ... " and he had Spadge on his face, his left arm twisted behind him, groaning and still wriggling. Rocky gave the arm another twist and Spadge yelled and lay still.

Rocky held it for a moment, then he panted, "Got him, Chick! Got Spadge!"

"Right! We're comin'."

"Let him go – we'll have ter clear off. There's too many of them," hissed the Nabber. "They're comin' – they're goin' ter do us!"

But Rocky gave another twist to Spadge's arm and said, "Tell them ter get back, Spadge, or I'll break it," and Spadge shouted, "Go back, Chick – he's breaking me arm!"

Chick's Lot and the tiddlers stopped, not knowing what to do. Then Chick shouted, "Lerrim go or I'll get the Sissler!"

"Forget that!" shouted Rocky. "Der's no Sissler! I know about Bobby Sissley! Know all about him! *And* the deri! Know all about it! What I've really come about! Yer leave him alone or I'll make sure the scuffers know about the Rialto!"

"Yer goin' ter grass?"

"Could grass – about yer deri and the trannies and the tiddlers … "

"Yer don't grass on us and get away with it!"

"Not grassin'. Not if yer lay off Bobby Sissley – and us!"

"Grass and we finish yer!"

"Not worth grassin' on," Rocky replied contemptuously. "Scuffers'll be on ter yer anyway. And yer keep off *my* deri or we'll take yer out – got it?"

"Got it?" yelled Suzie.

"Shurrup, Suzie! Get your lot away, Chick, or I'll break his arm!"

"Geroff, Chick," pleaded Spadge. "Geroff quick."

"I'm breakin' his arm *now*!" Rocky shouted to encourage them and Chick gave an order and they started moving back with Chick shouting, "Get yer for this, Rocky O'Rourke – won't ferget yer ever fer this!"

Inspired by Rocky's victory – and very relieved – the Cats joined in – "Go and take a walk on the Mersey!" shouted the Nabber, and Beady recommended that they shouldn't stop till they got to Blackpool. And it was then that Suzie shouted something she shouldn't have – and threw her half brick. It must have reached somebody because there

172

was a loud yell from the darkness.

"Out!" Rocky shouted and he let go of Spadge's arm and started running. But suddenly his foot was grabbed from behind and he fell flat on his face, kicking but not able to move and Spadge was shouting, "Chick! I've got him, Chick!"

Don't panic – think. McMahon's words went through Rocky's mind and he relaxed and then jack-knifed and grabbed the first pieces of Spadge that he could find, which happened to be his ears. Rocky pulled at them and Spadge shrieked and let go of Rocky's foot and as Rocky scrambled to his feet he saw that a small, dark figure was dancing on Spadge's back like a fiend and shouting, "Bad!" It was Suzie. Rocky lifted her up and started running with Suzie kicking and shouting, "Bad!"

The Cats raced along Joseph Terrace, past the pub and the off-licence and stopped, panting and safe, on Princes Boulevard. Billy was sweating and his legs trembling with the effort of cycling.

"Hi – we done them!" said Rocky.

"*You* done them, Rocky," said Little Chan.

"Wur'd yer learn all that stuff from but?" asked the Nabber, impressed. "That's wrestlin' stuff!"

"The scuffer – he showed me!"

"Have ter hand it ter yer," said the Nabber. "Yer did them."

"Did them!" echoed Suzie.

"Hi – come on!" And they went along the Boulevard, elated and triumphant and fooling about.

In St Catherine's Square they eased up. A cold,

mean wind was blowing, but in the sky a lot of stars sparkled frostily, and in the lamplight outside number 3 the chromium on Joey's bike sparkled as well.

"Hi!" said the Nabber. "Look at this! This is something!"

"This is Japanese," said Little Chan. "It is a very expensive model."

"It's Joey's," said Rocky, torn between pride in Joey's bike and dislike of Joey, and forgetting that Suzie was listening.

"Your Joey must be rich," said Beady, admiringly.

"He's doin' all right," Rocky conceded, reluctantly, and got on to the bike, leaning forward to reach the handlebars. "I'm goin' ter get one of these as well sometime."

"When yer change the twenty?" asked the Nabber, sarcastically.

Somebody came towards them along the Square, carrying a plastic bag in which bottles clinked. It was Joey.

"Hi – you kids – geroff that bike!" he shouted, and then, "Oh, it's you, Rocky. Well, tell yer mates ter clear off."

"Not doin' nothin'," said Rocky, getting off the bike.

"Just clear them off."

Joey went into number 3 and the Cats stood back and considered the situation.

"Wouldn't leave that out here if it was mine," said the Nabber.

"That's up ter Joey," said Rocky.

"Could let his tyres down," suggested the Nabber.

"You leave them alone," said Rocky, fiercely. "If anybody lets Joey's tyres down, it'll be *me*."

They discussed the next thing to be done, which was cleaning out the hideout, but then Billy said, "What about the footy, but? Saturday? Chick's Lot'll not come now."

"Yer could ask," began Rocky, then changed his mind. "No, Billy. Better keep away from them. They'll want to take it out on somebody. If dey don't come on Saturday doesn't matter. We can just have a practice. And if they do come, we'll take them out again, right?"

Billy and Little Chan and Beady drifted off, Billy feeling very relieved that he didn't have to face Chick again, but the Nabber hung around and eventually said, "Have ter hand it ter yer, Rocky – yer *have* done Chick. Have ter tell yer – when yer left the Cats that time at the school and was goin' over ter Chick's Lot, I was goin' ter take the Cats over meself – but they didn't want me. Think they was right."

It didn't come easy to the Nabber to say this, and Rocky appreciated it. "Think nothin' of it," he said. "The Cats know der's a windbag about when dey hear the bag-pipes playin'."

"Come over in a razor-boat, didn't yer?"

"Got the cuts to prove it."

They stood together in the dark Square, looking

175

at Joey's bike. Rocky was reluctant to go home now that Joey was there.

"Goin' ter the bonfire? Guy Fawkes night?" he asked.

"Me dad's takin' me. Yer could come with us," offered the Nabber.

"Hi – that'd be smashin'. Have ter bring Suzie, but."

"No!" The Nabber staggered about, dragging his camouflage hat down over his face.

"Can't leave her, Nabber. But tell yer what – we could fasten her to a rocket."

"Yer on. See yer, anyway."

"See yer."

The electric fire was going full blast again and Mrs Flanagan and Joey sat one on either side of it. They had a glass of beer each and they were leaning forward engaged in serious conversation. That was unusual, and so was the way they stopped talking as soon as Rocky came in, and looked at him – rather nervously, he thought.

"Hello, luv," said Mrs Flanagan, very amiably. "Joey's back."

"Can see that." Rocky dropped on the sofa and glowered at the electric fire.

"How's things den?" Joey asked, in a friendly way, and Mrs Flanagan handed Rocky a packet of crisps as if it was a packet of gold dust. "Joey bought them," she said.

"This all there is?"

"There's some ham and pickles for later on."

There was a nervous silence broken only by the sound of Rocky crunching crisps and Joey rustling his newspaper. Something was going on that he didn't know about, Rocky thought.

"Nice ter have Joey back, in't it?" said his mother.

"No," said Rocky.

"What yer mean no?"

"When's he goin' back ter Canada?"

"He's not. He's stayin' and he's got every right to – this is his home!"

There was another silence and Rocky waited. Then Joey said, "Hear yer inter somethin', Rocky."

"Me? I'm not inter anything," and Rocky screwed up the empty crisp packet, beginning to understand things.

"But the scuffers took yer in – and there's the twenty … "

"Oh, that was all right – they clarified me … "

"But the twenty … "

"Didn't lift it nor nothin', but tell yer something, Joey," said Rocky, confidentially, seeing a way to fix Joey as he'd fixed Chick and Spadge. "It's yer bike. The scuffers is interested in it."

Joey dropped his paper and sat up. "What they say?"

"When they took me in – said there was a bike like yours in Prinney Boulevard outside an old man's house that was done that night – remember, mam?"

"Well – well, I think I remember … "

"They was interested. Didn't tell them nothin', but."

"Nothin' ter tell them." Joey sounded casual and drank some beer, but he looked worried.

"Course there's not!" exclaimed Mrs Flanagan. "The cheek! Don't you worry yourself, Joey. Now we'll have the ham and pickles and ... "

"Suzie not come in yet?" Rocky asked, suddenly realizing that she wasn't around.

"Was with you, wasn't she?"

She had been and Rocky thought she'd gone into number 3. He went quickly into his bedroom. It was empty and Suzie wasn't under either of the beds or in the cupboard and she *had* seen Joey and his bike.

"She's gone again!" he told his mother.

"Yer should of watched her!"

"Yer know she doesn't like Joey!" Rocky got his torch.

"What she not like *me* for?" asked Joey, aggrieved. "I've done her no harm!"

Suzie was in the hideout. She was sitting on the old settee, crying.

"Yer've done it again, Suzie," said Rocky, sitting down beside her. "What yer do it for?"

"Him back," sobbed Suzie.

"Not fer long. He'll be off again."

"Torn, Rocky," sobbed Suzie picking at the filling from the slashed sofa.

"Look, Suzie," said Rocky desperately, "I'll get the hideout put right. Got it, Suzie? And yer'll stop cryin' and stop runnin' off."

Suzie gave a last sob and smiled at him. "All right, Rocky."

"Right. We're goin' back. There's some crisps and some ham and some pickles. And yer don't need ter see Joey. And we're goin' ter the bonfire on Guy Fawkes and – well, come on!"

Joey's bike wasn't outside number 3 when they got back.

"Gone," said Suzie.

"Looks like it. Come on."

Mrs Flanagan turned from the fire, tearfully. "Yer should of left *her* where yer found her – Joey's gone because of her!" she said.

"No, he's not. Gone because I told him the scuffers were interested in him."

"Yer shouldn't of told him that then!"

"Had ter give him the warnin', didn't I?"

"Well – yer right. Poor Joey – they never let him alone!"

"He'll be fine – be over in Birkenhead with his pals now," and Rocky looked at the plates of ham and pickles on the table. "Ham and pickle butties," he suggested and his mother perked up a bit. "There's some blackcurrant tarts as well," she said, "and yer sure our Joey'll be all right, Rocky?"

Ferociously making butties, Rocky muttered, "Always all right is Joey."

"What yer sayin'?"

"Nothin'. Here." He handed her a butty, but at that moment she sat up straight, staring ahead. "I've got the intuitions," she whispered. "Somethin' awful."

Rocky and Suzie watched her anxiously. "What yer got them about?" Rocky asked, cautiously.

"Can't be Joey, can it?" Mrs Flanagan thought it over. "Could be Flanagan. Or your auntie Chrissie … " And she took a bite out of her butty and Rocky relaxed. "S'all right den – long as it's not me. Here, Suzie, that's your butty and switch the telly on."

Rocky enjoyed that evening. The food was good, Joey had gone and he'd fixed Chick's Lot and rescued the Sissleys. And he could spend the twenty and get the hideout cleaned up.

But then he thought maybe his mother's intuitions meant that the terrorist would be round again. But he couldn't really believe it. The terrorist hadn't been around for a long time. Must have given it up now. And it was footy tomorrow in Prinney Park – if Chick's Lot had the guts to turn up! And with the wingy refereeing and Bobbie Sissley playing, the Cats should win – they *would* win!

CHAPTER

17

IT was early when Rocky woke up next morning – well, it was half past nine and that was early for a Saturday. There was no sound from the other room, so he knew Suzie and his mother were still asleep and he got ready and went quietly along the passage and out into the Square. In his near-purple shirt, his football under his arm, he ran past Mrs Aber's towards Princes Boulevard. He would be early for the match, but he could do a bit of practice waiting for the others.

A car drew up by the kerb just ahead of him and the driver leaned towards him and opened the nearside door.

"Hi, son," he said. "Which way is it ter Hardman Street?"

Rocky went up to the car. "S'not far," he said, helpfully. "Yer go up here and then yer ... "

He was suddenly grabbed from behind and thrown into the car, his football bouncing away down the street. A man pushed in beside him and the door slammed and the car started off. Rocky struggled, but he couldn't get free. That hand was over his mouth again and he was pinned back against the seat between the driver and the man who'd grabbed him and he knew who *he* was. And nothing McMahon had taught him would help him now.

"Where d'yer want to stop?" asked the driver.

"Somewhere quiet." It was that hoarse, whispering voice.

Mr Oliver, with Rocky's football tucked under his one arm, knocked awkwardly on the door of Mrs Flanagan's living-room. There was no reply, so he knocked again and then heard somebody moving about inside. Then the door opened and Mrs Flanagan appeared in her dressing-gown and slippers. Behind her, Mr Oliver could see the bed with Suzie standing up on it in her nightdress.

"What's all this?" asked Mrs Flanagan.

"Sorry ter get yer up – is Rocky in?"

"He'll be in bed still. What yer want him for?"

"Found his football outside Mrs Aber's."

"Typical!" said Mrs Flanagan. "He thinks they come through the post free! I'll murder him!" And she came out to try the door to Rocky's bedroom. But there was no sign of Rocky.

"He's gone off," said Mrs Flanagan.

"That's all right," said the wingy. "He'll be in Prinney Park – we've got a match on." But he looked worried as he went away, and he could hear Suzie screaming and Mrs Flanagan shouting at her.

The car stopped in a lane between two rows of houses.

"This do?" The driver switched off the engine and it was very quiet – nobody about.

Rocky was twisted round and looked into the face with those staring eyes that had no pity in them.

"Where did he go?"

Rocky pulled at the hand over his face, making protesting, grunting noises.

The hand was released. "Let's have it then."

Rocky's mouth was so dry with fear that he couldn't speak at first, but his mind was working fast. He didn't want to clat on anybody, but he knew he would have to and the man *had* said to give his address. And he'd said there would be help. But Rocky had a feeling that nothing could save him from the terrorist.

"I said where'd he go?" And Rocky was punched back against the car seat.

Rocky made his mind up. He was in it now. He'd have to play it as it came. "Tell yer," he mumbled, sounding terrified – and he wasn't play-acting. "The Oaks. Sefton Drive."

"Know it, Sean?"

For answer, the driver started the car and the terrorist said, "If yer lyin' I'll make yer sorry yer were born." And then, "Yer could have told me before and saved a lot of trouble."

Rocky said nothing. He watched the streets passing, trying to keep alert for any chance to escape. He heard the driver say, "Yer'll not find him there. He's not stayin' around waitin' for yer."

"Doesn't know I'm comin'. The pigs moved him

to a safe house and he thinks he's safe, the dirty grass. Thinks he'll stay put till the next team comes over from Belfast and then he'll grass on *them*. But he won't. He won't grass again."

It had started to rain and the driver switched on the windscreen wipers. Rocky watched them going backwards and forwards monotonously, with a slight squeak each time. The driver took a cigarette from a packet beside him and lit it. "If it's a safe house why did he give this kid the address?" he asked through a cloud of smoke.

And after a moment's pause, the terrorist said, thoughtfully, "Yes, why did he?" He twisted Rocky's face round to him. "Why did he?"

Rocky spoke quickly. "I saved his life – saved him from you. He said ter me, 'I owe yer my life, take this num … ' " he corrected himself, " 'take this address. Any time – any time yer need help … ' "

The two men thought about this, then the driver said, "Still don't like it. Yer walkin' into a trap. Look, why don't we give this up and get a hit man over ter do the job?"

"Because he grassed on us and *I'm* settlin' with him. What yer stopped for?"

"This is Sefton Drive."

It was a street of old, respectable-looking houses set back behind stone walls and shrubberies; a quiet street with one or two cars parked and a woman hurrying past under an umbrella. Half-way down, two workmen had the cover off a man-hole and were looking down into it, watched by another two sitting in a British Telecom van. Rocky thought about the Cats playing footy in Prinney Park – not so far away – and wished he was with them.

"Don't like it," the driver repeated.

"Yer don't have to. Which house is it?" the terrorist asked Rocky.

"Don't know – honest, I don't ... "

The terrorist hit him across the head so hard he saw flecks of light.

"Let the lad alone, Steve," said the driver. "Why *should* he know? And we can't sit here talking. I'll drive down – keep yer eyes open ... "

The car started again. One side of Rocky's face was numb, but his mind began to clear and he started to get angry. He hadn't been beaten by Jim Simpson and he wouldn't be beaten by the terrorist – even though he was a lot more dangerous. Do him, he thought, I'll do him. He deserves it.

He heard them saying it was the house with the brown door and the steps up to it and that they'd drive round a bit and come back, and he heard the driver saying that they should give it up because the Telecom workers could be scuffers and it could be a trap, and the terrorist telling him to shut up.

They stopped again. Rocky recognized where they were – on the road round Sefton Park, just beside the lake. If he could have escaped from the car, he could have run off into the trees and been safe, but there was no chance of that. The terrorist sat still and silent beside him.

"Yer goin' on with it?" asked the driver and lit

another cigarette, and Rocky saw that his hands were trembling.

The terrorist didn't answer. He got out of the car and pulled Rocky after him and pushed him into the back seat.

"What's yer name?"

"Bill Stickers," retorted Rocky, defiantly.

For a moment they looked straight at each other, then the terrorist smiled. It was an unnerving smile, because it had no feeling in it. "Yer've got guts," he said. "And yer'll need them. Ever done a paper round, Bill Stickers? Yer goin' ter do one. We're stoppin' at the end of that street and yer gettin' out ter do yer paper round. This is yer bag – full of papers, see? And there's somethin' else in it – a bit heavier. Yer'll walk down that street to the house with the brown door and yer'll go up the steps and yer'll ring the bell. Can manage that, Bill Stickers, can't yer? If *he* comes out, just drop the bag and yer'll have three minutes – just three minutes, Bill Stickers – to get away, then the house'll go up, because I'll detonate the bomb in that bag, see? If he doesn't come out – well, yer can go on putting papers through the doors down the street and we'll pick yer up at the bottom. We'll take the bag and we'll see yer all right. And we'll not bother yer any more." He put the strap of the bag round Rocky's neck then he took a rifle from the floor of the car. "That's if yer do as yer told. But you try anythin' on and I'll blow yer brains out – and yer've got some brains ter blow out, haven't yer, Bill Stickers?"

Rocky scowled at the man. What did he take him for – a nit? Whatever happened the terrorist would get rid of him – he knew too much. He'd go up with the bomb or be shot in the back. But he didn't give the man any lip – that would just get him knocked about. He just made his mind up – he was coming out of this alive.

The car door shut behind him as he started walking, rain blowing into his face. He tried to walk casually, but it wasn't easy – the bag was heavy and his head was throbbing. The Telecom men – if they *were* scuffers – didn't seem interested in him. He could hear them talking and one of them laughing. But the rain helped to clear his head and he took a deep breath, walking slowly, conscious of the gun pointed at his back.

When he turned into the pathway of the house, he knew that, for a few moments, he was hidden by the garden wall and the terrorist couldn't see him, and he could pause for a moment and think – but not for too long because if the terrorist got impatient or suspicious he could just detonate that bomb. The steps at the front of the house seemed a long way away and very steep, and once he got to the top the terrorist would have him in the sights of his rifle. Rocky made his plans and started slowly towards the steps, taking his time, breathing easily, getting ready for what he had to do.

Going up the steps was the longest walk he'd ever taken and when he got to the top he carefully pulled the strap of the bag off his shoulder and laid the bag very gently on the top step, and took a newspaper out of it. It was a *Liverpool Echo*. He heard a motor bike go down the road and again he heard one of the British Telecom men laughing. He wished they were the scuffers and would help him, but he didn't think they were. He took a deep breath, pushed the paper through the letter-box, making a clatter, pressed the door-bell and heard its sharp ring. But nothing happened. Three minutes he had, the terrorist said. That must be one gone. He felt very lonely and vulnerable. Better forget about the white-haired man and start running, he thought, but then he heard footsteps behind the door, a key being turned in the lock and he braced himself. And it all happened together. The door opened a crack and he saw the white-haired man looking at him and he hissed, "Bomb – gerout!" and had an impression of the man stumbling away from the door before he threw the bag into the bushes at one side of the steps and dropped over the other side himself into more bushes, scrambling through them on his hands and knees, desperate to put some space between himself and the bag before the bomb was detonated. But the ground started moving under him and there was an orange light all round him and something pushed him from behind into the trunk of a tree and he was deafened by the noise of an explosion.

He lay still under a hail of falling branches and stones and fragments of glass and a cloud of dust. The Telecom men were shouting and he could hear rifle shots. He got to his feet, pushing his way through the bushes, and when he turned to look back he saw the whole front of the house slowly slipping down and disintegrating, and he started running across a lawn, scrambled over a wall into another garden and got out on to the street.

He ran like a deer that had got on to a motorway by mistake, his eyes dull with fear and his mind frozen. Even when he got to the busy streets he didn't see or hear anything. He didn't hear the woman who shouted, "Who d'yer think yer pushin'?" or the man who said, "He's goin' ter break the sound barrier!" or the man who replied, "Break his neck first, won't he?" But his head seemed to be filled with the sound of police sirens.

It was the wingy who finally stopped him, stepping out of Mrs Aber's gate in front of him and saying, "Here – Rocky!"

Rocky stared at him, not knowing who he was at first, then he dropped against Mrs Aber's wall, hardly able to draw his breath, his heart pounding, his legs feeling as though they were going to give way. He couldn't take in what Mr Oliver was saying – something about a football game, something about the Cats, something about his face. Then he felt Mr Oliver's hand grasping his shoulder reassuringly and he began to feel better and his breathing got easier and he heard Mr Oliver say, "What's up wid yer, Rocky?"

"Can't tell yer," Rocky gasped. "Can't tell yer."

"Now look – it's not a scrap with Chick's Lot, so what is it?" Rocky twisted away from him, leaning

heavily on the wall and shaking his head. "Can't –
can't … " Then he looked up. "Listen!"

Mr Oliver turned sharply to look towards Princes
Boulevard as a fire engine, and then another, then a
police car, then an ambulance went past with lights
and sirens going.

"Think they got … " Rocky mumbled and then
muttered something that Mr Oliver couldn't make
out. Then he said, "Yer last terrorist … think they
got … but I promised … and the white-haired … was
he … killed?"

He's raving, thought Mr Oliver. "Yer'll come in
and sit down," he said.

Rocky shook his head again. "No – doesn't matter
– all over – finished … doesn't matter. Like some
water."

Nothing had tasted so good to Rocky as the water
the wingy brought out to him. As he drank it, the
cold, damp wind cooled his face.

Mr Oliver watched him anxiously and then made
his mind up. "It's ter do with them young fellers I
took in and that business down at the police station,
isn't it? I'm getting McMahon – you wait here."

"No – don't. Doesn't matter – all over. And
McMahon'll know – and the sergeant." And it
suddenly got through to Rocky that it *was* all over
and the terrorist wouldn't come after him again.
Would always be a nightmare, but, he thought.
Then he grinned at Mr Oliver – a painful grin
because of his bruised face. But he appreciated Mr
Oliver's concern and thought he might as well get

190

something more out of it. "That twenty, Mr Oliver? Can yer change it now?"

Mr Oliver got angry. "Another mystery! It's all mystery with you! Yer don't deserve any help ... " and he stumped away towards the door of Mrs Aber's flats, then he stumped back again. "Right," he said. "The twenty was cleared and I've just collected the rents for the flats so I'll change it. It'll have to be fivers."

"That's great, Mr Oliver! Great!"

While the wingy was getting the fivers, Rocky looked round the Square. Was all right was the Square with its abandoned garden and the builder's hut and the old car and Barbie's grave. Was all right – now. And seeing the old vicarage he decided he'd get the hideout put right straight away. Get the Cats together ...

"Hi, Mr Oliver – what happened? Chick's Lot turn up for the match?"

"More than *you* did! And they played like they was crazy. Never seen nothing like it. But yer don't need ter worry. I stopped the Nabber takin' over and the Cats won – mainly because of Bobbie Sissley – played like a dream. Said it was ter thank yer for helpin' her brother. Now what's *that* all about?"

"Tell yer sometime."

Mr Oliver watched him pocketing the fivers and sensed that everything was all right with Rocky now.

"Here, what about the twenty, then?" he asked.

"Bring it round, Mr Oliver. Honest. Ternight."

"Yer'd better or me rents'll be short." And he watched Rocky going happily, but a bit shakily, towards number 3.

Then Rocky turned round but kept on walking, backwards.

"Mr Oliver – you a senior citizen?"

"Me? A senior – how old d'yer think I am?" asked Mr Oliver indignantly.

"Sorry. Ferget it then!"

In the passage there was a fantastic smell of roasting chicken and Rocky decided it must be from Ellen-from-upstairs. It made him feel hollow inside and he burst into the living-room to find some food. Then he stopped in amazement. The smell was coming from the oven, there were new bright orange curtains at the window and his mother was standing in front of the fire and looking at herself in the mirror and she was wearing a pink suit and hat and Suzie was squashed into a corner of the sofa, absolutely awed.

Mrs Flanagan twirled round. "What yer think of this?" she asked. She didn't notice his bruised face and she didn't ask where he'd been all morning.

Rocky dropped on to the sofa, exhausted. "It's Buckingham Palace," he muttered.

"I got it for the wedding – Ellen's."

"Wur'd the money come from, but?"

"Come from Flanagan. Wur'd you think?"

Suzie put her hand up and touched his face. "Hurt, Rocky," she whispered and started sobbing.

"What's she on about?" demanded Mrs Flanagan from the cooker where she was involved with plates and chicken and chips.

"S'nothin', mam. Yer gettin' chicken, Suzie," he added, "and I'm gettin' yer a present. And we're goin' to the bonfire. Got it? So shurrup!"

Suzie wiped her nose with the back of her hand and smiled. "Chicken – shurrup," she said.

As they ate chicken and chips and peas with the telly going, Mrs Flanagan, still in her pink suit and flowered hat, said, "I told Ellen I'd do the tea for her wedding because she was very good when yer had that fall down the Steps. I'll get some ham for the sandwiches but she'll bring the cake. And I'm gettin' some sausage rolls from Pa Richardson ... "

"And pies," muttered Rocky, his mouth full of chicken.

"That's right – pies."

"And pizzas."

"Yes – pizzas. I'll cut them up."

"And beans." Rocky was grinning to himself.

"Beans? What yer mean beans?" Mrs Flanagan demanded indignantly.

"Well, yer always get beans."

"*Beans?* For a *weddin'*? Are yer daft?" Then getting suspicious, "Here – you takin' the mickey?"

"No, mam. Honest. What yer done with the old curtains?"

"They're in the bottom of the cupboard." She looked round the room distractedly. "This place'll have ter be cleaned up as well ... "

Rocky didn't hear any more, because there was a news flash on the television about a house being blown up in Sefton Drive. No casualties, but two men arrested. That's it, he thought. It's over. And he fell back on the sofa and went into a deep sleep.

He was wakened by his mother shaking him and complaining, "Yer haven't finished yer chicken! And it cost plenty."

"Give it – Suzie," he muttered, and fell asleep again.

Next day he wakened to the quiet of a Sunday morning and lay in the semi-darkness feeling frightened without knowing why. Then it all came back to him and relief surged through him. He got out of bed and went quietly into the next room. He could just make out the two humps on the bed – one large, one small – his mother and Suzie. Stealthily he got the mirror from above the mantelpiece and examined his face. There was a slightly purplish bruise down one side that went right round his eye. He felt rather proud of it – a black eye was proof he'd been in the wars.

He put the mirror back and was just getting the old curtains from the cupboard when Suzie sat up and said, "Rocky!"

"Sssh!" he hissed, but then some voices outside started shouting. "Rocky! Hi, Rocky!" and his mother stirred, muttering angrily, "What's all that noise?"

"Just goin' ter find out," he said hastily, and

escaped with the curtains and Suzie scampering after him.

When he opened the front door and stood there with the curtains draped round him and his purplish eye and Suzie behind him in her nightdress watching them suspiciously, the Cats were stunned.

"Must be having delusions," said Beady.

"Who did yer eye?" asked Billy.

"And what yer let us down for yesterday? We waited hours for yer – yer messed up everythin'!" the Nabber said angrily.

"We only waited quarter of an hour," Little Chan put in.

"Will youse keep quiet," said Rocky. "Me mam'll come out ter yer."

"Well, where were you?"

"I know," said Beady. "It has ter be – the terrorist again!"

"That's right," said Rocky. "It was – he got me ... "

"Try something else," the Nabber retorted. "The scuffers got the terrorist yesterday – it was on the telly last night – he was blowing a house up – we heard the bang ... "

"Look," said Rocky fiercely, "I know all that – I was there – I'm tellin' yer ... I was on me way ter the Park when he got me. He made me plant the bomb – I was nearly killed – there was stones falling all round and ... "

"Well, that's funny – they didn't even mention yer," said the Nabber sarcastically.

"They wouldn't – the scuffers wouldn't tell them – has ter be secret or they'll send another terrorist to get *me* – 'cos I messed their plans up … "

"Ah, come off it!"

"I'll do you, Nabber Neville!"

Mrs Flanagan appeared in the passage in her dressing-gown. "Will you clear that lot off and come in here!" she shouted.

"Listen," Rocky said quietly, when she'd disappeared, "I'll tell youse all about it. See youse at the hideout – we'll clean it up – bring anything yer can. I've got these curtains for the sofa – right?"

"Now then, lads," said a voice behind them. "Want a private word with Rocky." It was the sergeant from Larkspur Lane and when the Cats had moved out of earshot, but were still watching curiously, he said, "Came to see yer were all right after the business yesterday – would have called straight away, but Mr Oliver came down to tell us yer'd got home all right. How yer feeling?"

"Me? I'm fine – just me eye … "

"I can see it's a shiner – lucky that's all yer got. Now, Rocky, yer know yer'll get no public credit for what yer did – got to be secret for everybody's sake – but I wanted yer ter know what yer did is appreciated – in certain circles. All right?"

"S'all right. Think nothin' of it."

"Well remember – if yer in any trouble, any time, yer know where to come." He was turning away when Rocky suddenly shouted, "Hi – sergeant. Have yer got any old furniture yer don't want?"

"Old furniture? Think I run a junk shop? Wait a bit, though. There's an old table with a broken leg been around the place for years – yer could have that. Yer'll have ter collect it. That be any good?"

"Great! Be down for it this mornin'."

"What yer want a table for?"

Rocky grinned. "Can't tell yer. It's a secret as well, see? Anyway, youse owe me, so if yer come across anything else, I'll have it."

This interview, together with their visit to the police station to collect one old table, went a long way in convincing the Cats that there had to be *some* truth in Rocky's story after all and maybe he *was* a bit of a hero (Billy had always thought so), and when the hideout was cleaned out and they sat down to a brew-up and listened to the story again – in detail – not even the Nabber expressed any disbelief.

18

TWO days later, the Cats Gang and Suzie were skating along Princes Boulevard – well, Suzie was tottering.

"Can't!" she shouted. "Can't!"

"Keep yerself up – don't lean forwards. Lean back!"

Suzie leant back and fell on her bottom. She sat there, tears rolling down her face. "Don't like it!"

Rocky swirled back to her. "Yer'll have ter like it! Them skates cost money!" Rocky heaved her up. "Come on – hang on ter me arm."

They turned towards St Catherine's Square and Beady, Billy, the Nabber and Little Chan stood watching them. "It's Torvill and Dean," said the Nabber.

Then a man in a black coat and black hat with a partly grey beard and half-moon spectacles came up to them.

"Can you tell me where I can find Rocky O'Rourke?" he asked.

"That's him with the red hair," said the Nabber. "The one hangin' on ter the little girl for support."

"The one disappearin' into the sunset," said Billy,

doing a turn on his bike.

"The one headin' for the Mersey Tunnel," said Little Chan.

"You're his friends?" asked the man.

"That's right, mister. We're the Skate Gang – smells fishy, don't it?" And Beady collapsed against the wall, laughing at his own joke.

"Will you get him to come here?"

The man was so impressive that the Cats were silent and then Beady shouted for Rocky. He left Suzie sitting on the pavement and came back and stood in front of the man.

"Rocky," said the man, "this is for you. With my thanks." And he handed Rocky a brown envelope. Rocky looked at him. "What's it?" he asked.

"For you."

Rocky didn't know who he was, but there was something familiar about him. If you took away the hat and the beard ... he could be the man with the white hair!

"Hi, mister!" he shouted as the man got into a car, but he drove off.

"What yer got?" asked the Nabber.

Rocky opened the envelope, then he shouted, "The nit! He's done it again! A fifty! I'll never change it!"

"This is a serial, in't it?" said the Nabber. "It'll be a hundred next time!"

"Could easily be," agreed Rocky, pushing his hand through his red hair in excitement. "Could have ter do somethin' even more dangerous another time. Yer can't tell when yer get into these things. Listen – I'm takin' this down ter the scuffers now to get it clarified, then I'll get the wingy ter change it and then we'll – well come on! Beady and Little Chan help Billy with his bike down the Steps and Nabber take one of Suzie's arms – I'll take the other and we'll carry her down … "

They clattered down the Steps with Suzie swinging between Rocky and Nabber and shrieking at the top of her voice.

"Shurrup, Suzie!" Rocky panted. "Will yer shurrup!"